HAND-PAINTED TEXTILES

HAND-PAINTED TEXTILES

A Practical Guide to the Art of Painting on Fabric

Sarah Campbell

HERBERT PRESS

HERBERT PRESS
Bloomsbury Publishing Plc
50 Bedford Square, London, WC1B 3DP, UK
29 Earlsfort Terrace, Dublin 2, Ireland

BLOOMSBURY, HERBERT PRESS and the Herbert Press logo
are trademarks of Bloomsbury Publishing Plc

First published in Great Britain in 2023

A catalogue record for this book is available from the British Library
Library of Congress Cataloguing-in-Publication data has been applied for

ISBN: 978-1-78994-064-0; eBook: 978-1-78994-062-6

2 4 6 8 10 9 7 5 3 1

Typeset and designed by Laura Woussen
Printed and bound in China by Toppan Leefung Printing

FSC www.fsc.org MIX Paper from responsible sources FSC® C104723

p. 70: Cueva de las Manos (Cave of Hands) © Alex Treadway / Getty Images.

For Jodie, Quino and Paco

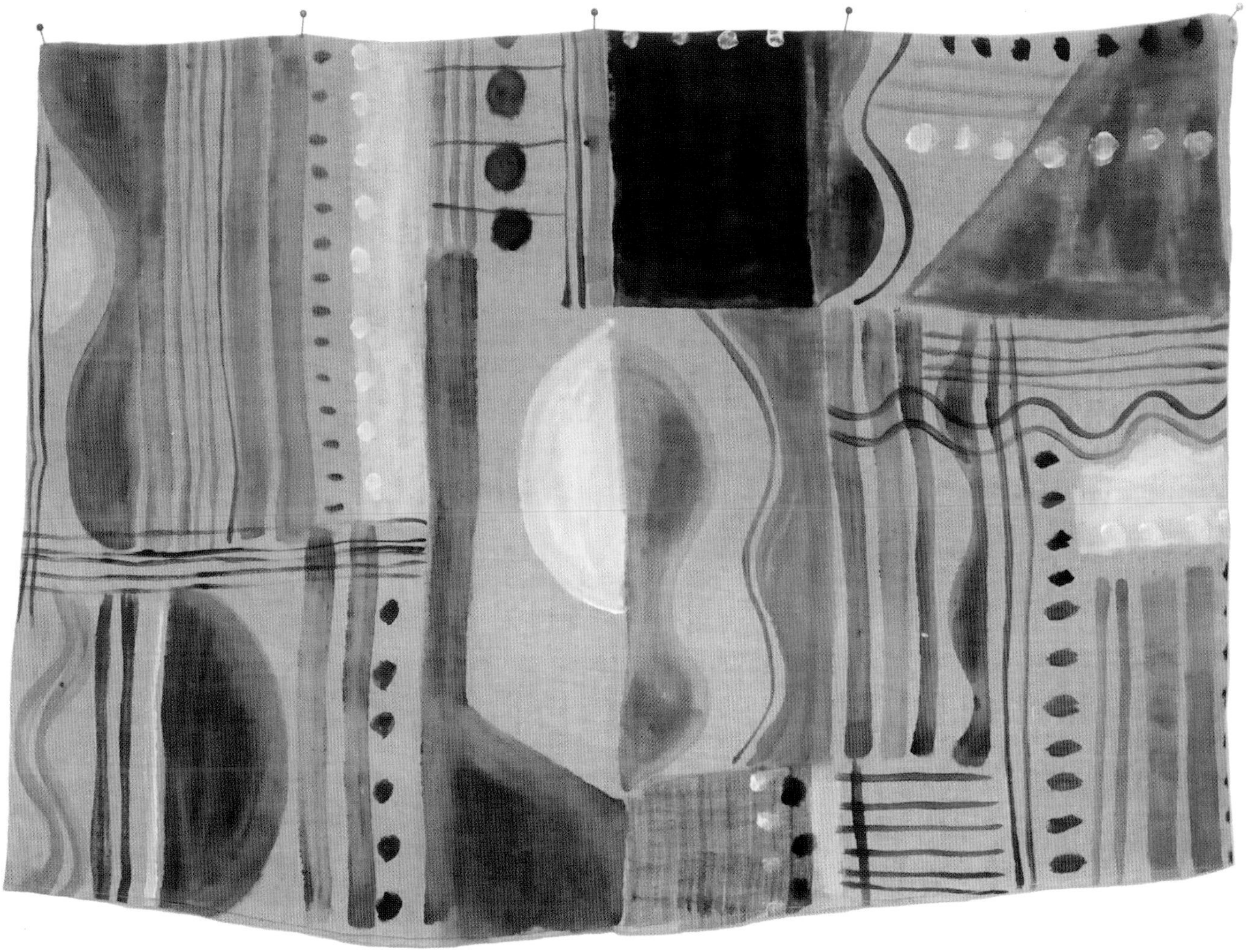

CONTENTS

INTRODUCTION

The world is full of pattern and design – applied, implied and integral within nature. We humans need its colour and the fascination, reassurance and reflection it brings. I love to paint and am endlessly intrigued by pattern and how it works; these are the fundamental strands of my creative and professional life as a decorative applied artist, working within the industry. This book sets that commercial process aside to explore and describe the application of colour and pattern by hand, directly onto fabric.

The nature of making a design for print production requires, at its heart, the organisation of marks and motifs into a repeat that can be printed on large rotary, flatbed or hand screen-printing machines. Of course, this organisation is the subplot of a pattern repeat. What sells the cloth is the colour, scale and content – in a way, the dream.

During my long career as a textile designer, since the mid-1960s, the greatest amount of time has been spent inventing, painting and colouring patterns in repeat on paper for commercially printed textiles. More recently, I've expanded my horizons into taking direct action, hand-painting unique and decorative pieces onto the cloth itself. Naturally, the two pursuits share a great deal – an understanding of colour, distribution, motif, scale and so on – but their differences are equally important.

Above Cote d'Azur being commercially printed.

PAINTING ON FABRIC: STARTING OUT

Painting straight onto fabric is a very different experience – from me to you, in a manner of speaking, with no middlemen or commercial production issues. Everything is unique, and for commissioned items such as this upholstered chair (below) and the silk jacket (opposite), the placing of the patterns and colours in relation to the form and usage is in my hands. The beauty is that the pattern doesn't have to repeat – there can be just one bird or just one square, if it's in the right place.

Designs destined for production have a long journey – often literally across continents – from my hand to those of the final customer via the manufacturer, the cloth merchant, the engraver, the printworks, the colour-matcher, the agent and the retailer. And then they're subject to the wielding of the mighty scissors – I have no say in how they're used, so I need to ensure that the fabric will withstand all the cutting and sewing and still be recognisable as the pattern I invented on day one!

Left The tiny dots painted at the cuff edge of George's fancy jacket make a great contrast to the otherwise ebullient jungle scene, and are a seductive detail when sitting at table or holding hands! You can take a closer look at these pieces later on in the book (see page 102).

Painting directly onto fabric can be a risky business, full of chance encounters with wayward inks, unintended splodges and unforeseen 'effects'. But along with these comes the tremendous fun and liberation of planning bespoke pattern making. Writing a favourite poem on a scarf or painting a vibrant coloured border onto a dress, making a special cushion for a friend or a summer skirt for a customer – the content, pattern and colour placement makes things particular, outweighing any potential disasters. In these instances, the form and its function are in my hands.

Over recent years I've experimented with and invented various techniques and methods for painting on textiles; teaching myself and many others too. Recently, at a short course I was teaching at Morley College about painting on fabric, a student commented, 'You should write a book about this.' I answered, a little nervously, 'I am!' This book expands on my story: how I do it, what to expect and how you can do it too. I can't teach you how to draw, but I can show you how to paint on fabric, to experiment with techniques to make patterns on cloth and to think about how pattern works. This is not a book about rigid rules to stick to, but rather one of examples, proposals and possibilities, instances and encouragement.

Students often tell me they can't draw, they don't know where to start, or they feel constrained and hesitant when faced with a blank surface. To make pattern, you don't necessarily need to be able to draw. At its heart, pattern is largely about the rhythm: the building up and organisation of marks. You do, however, need to understand the concept of accumulation and the importance of composition and colour distribution. If you love pattern and cloth, want to experiment and learn about hand-painting, then this is the book for you!

When painting, I need to be able to feel the pressure of the brush, to be sensitive to the timing of the mark and the rhythm of its repetition, and to let these things feed back to me. I admit, I talk to my work all the time as I try to get it into shape; the marks, the drawing, the balance, the harmony, the structure, the colours, the content – they're all part of the dialogue. I often tell my students to let their work talk back to them, to listen to the conversation back and forth between the eye, the paper and the hand.

Far Left Traditional pieced quilt, cut and made from printed fabrics from my 'FreshPicked' collection for Free Spirit Fabrics USA 2022.

Bottom Left On my friend's chair I imagined a blue bird peeping over her shoulder, whistling a soft song.

FIRST PRINCIPLES

Before starting any project, make your work area (however small and modest) as pleasant as you can. Give yourself enough light, space and time to set things out nicely so you can enjoy the doing of the work! If you haven't painted on fabric before, you might like to start by practising your mark making with the various brushes and tools described in the next section (see page 14). As you'll see, these tools are a great way into experiencing painting, organising mark making and forming patterns.

I always use inks and paints that can be heat-set with a hot dry iron on the reverse at the end of the project. Once set, the cloth can be washed by hand to rinse out any loose colour on the surface, and then pressed again with a steam iron. But, in fact, 'finished' pieces can be revisited, as I will describe (see page 143), and overpainted and improved as you see fit. My calico and cotton hand-painted garments have all been washed in the machine at thirty degrees; I wash the linen items kindly by hand, and again, iron when damp.

The chosen fabric needs to be stretched and pinned to make an even, stable surface. You can be quite muscular with the pinning – by the time cloth (even silk) reaches you, it's had a hard life being woven, washed, pulled and rolled, so it won't mind an extra tug.

I either pin directly onto my wooden worktable with paper or old fabric beneath, or I use a 10mm (3/8in) foam board as my surface (of course, any drawing board will do). Apart from avoiding pinholes in the table, the advantage of using a board is that you can prop it up as you go along to give you some perspective on your progress, and it's easy to set it aside while you have dinner. And when your work is finished, you have the opportunity to look at it from a distance and in the vertical plane, which is always instructive! I generally have a few boards on the go, acting as extra studio walls.

As very wet paint can cause the foam board to warp, it's a good idea to cover it with a thin plastic sheet, wrapped around tightly and secured on the reverse. A polythene dust sheet from a DIY merchant is cheap and will go a long way; it can be wiped clean too, but it's not advisable to iron on. With clean water, kitchen towel or a cotton rag at the ready, and whatever tools and colours you can muster, you're ready to paint!

You'll need to practise and get the hang of how your paints and inks are working for you. They're affected by temperature and humidity, as well as the cloth used, so it's very tricky to prescribe exactly how much water you'll want to use to thin your paint, how quickly it may dry or how far it may spread on the fabric. This is one reason why a trial run is always a good idea when you're starting out; another is the fun of just seeing what occurs. Painting on fabric, as I've said, can be unpredictable; 'mistakes' can happen. Very often, spills can be mopped up and thus removed quickly with kitchen towel, but sometimes one just has to go with it, incorporate the mess and embrace the experience – even somehow to make a virtue of it.

When you come to draw your design out onto fabric, you can use an auto-fade pen as a guide; the marks will disappear of their own accord without a trace. But beware – some can fade to invisibility very quickly! Pens do vary, so check yours first in order not to lose your carefully drafted lines. I remember one evening, at the start of my painting on fabric investigations, diligently drawing out some lettering that I wanted to paint the next morning, only to discover it had all vanished by the time I got up!

Above Here, I managed to disguise some very disappointing splurging shapes with a sharp line painted on when all was dry: happily, our eyes tend to focus on that clear black line, ignoring the spread beneath!

I OFTEN TELL MY STUDENTS TO LET THEIR WORK TALK BACK TO THEM

THE TOOLS OF MY TRADE

It's important to know your tools and get them to work with and for you. Such a lot of pattern making and painting is dependent on the simple fact that different implements make different marks. One can make marks with various items, from a twig to a feather, a toothbrush to the edge of a piece of cardboard to a length of string – the list goes on. These can all be instructive, informative and fun adventures.

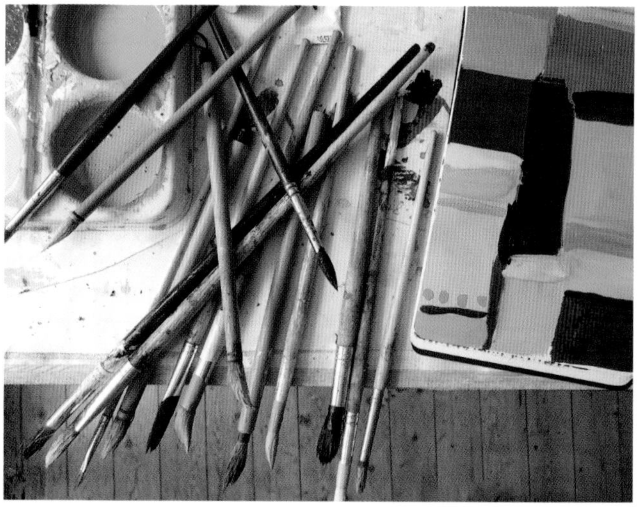

Primarily, I love to paint: to have control over the application of colour and form and to build a pattern or surface with confidence. I love the tools of my trade and, above all, I value my brushes. A good friendly brush – one that holds paint well, is responsive, versatile and moves with a firm spring – is worth having and keeping. Having said that, I can be merciless with paintbrushes and wear out my favourites far too quickly. The old warriors can then be used for mixing up new paint colours.

Right I love doing these experiments – here's what a bunch of palm fibre can do on paper.

PAINT AND INK

For works painted on fabric I always use products that can be heat-set by being hot-ironed on the reverse of the cloth. The paint or ink manufacturers advise the time needed for this, but I like to take longer. A good rule is to iron until the surface is too hot to touch by hand. I often use this time as a sort of meditation on the work itself.

The heat ensures the colour is fixed and retains its density when washed and also when exposed to sunlight. These are not dyes and inks that need to be steam-set or fixed with additives. I use a variety of different makes, all of which I mix together in a rather cavalier way.

Inks for silk and fabric painting are looser and runnier than the paints, and are often of a brighter hue. The paints are easier to control but can sometimes lack luminosity, so there are pluses and minuses to each.

Other variables when painting are the quality of the cloth used and the temperature and humidity in the atmosphere in your room and on the day. There are commercial mediums available to extend the paints or lighten the colours, but I mostly just use water for this.

Tip

An old washing-up liquid bottle, or similar, filled with clean water is a very handy tool when mixing paint: with a little squeeze you can easily control the amount of water you're adding to the mixture, and keep your other water pots just for cleaning your brushes.

FABRICS

I always try to source fabrics that have no applied surface finish – such as a glaze or conditioner; if I'm not sure, I wash and iron the cloth before I start. Several art and craft supply shops sell cloth ready to paint, and very simple and cheap unbleached calicoes are usually good to use straight away.

Older and vintage pieces – bedsheets, pillowcases and tablecloths, for example – are also an intriguing and valuable fabric source. They often provide an interesting surface, well-matured by a life of laundering – though, if washing again before painting, use no fabric conditioner in the rinse.

Other than basic calico, I use different plain cottons – poplin and other simple weaves and surfaces – pretty well anything that comes my way! Linen makes a beautiful surface to paint on, especially for upholstery, but it can be costly – it's worth looking out for bargains such as offcuts, ends of lines and deadstock.

I can't recommend fabrics with a large nylon or man-made content, but some viscose mixes are great and have a good drape. It really is a question of experimenting. And, with all fabrics, it's worth sparing a piece of the cloth as a trial to see how the colour behaves. There is a short list of materials, fabrics and inks at the back of this book for your reference (see page 176).

Note

I refer to calico throughout which, in the US, is also known as muslin.

Above Painting on gingham can be fun.

PAINTING TOOLS

These are some of the brushes – both foam and whisker, as I call them – and other tools that I use.

Rectangular Foam Brushes

Using a foam brush is a simple and cheap way of applying colour. The flat rectangular shapes come in several sizes. Marks made depend on the amount and viscosity of the paint used and the pressure exerted when painting – experiments are necessary! These brushes do not require the user to be able to draw 'artistically' in order to be effective in pattern and mark making.

Foam brushes

- Can hold a lot of colour/paint
- Can sustain the making of a long mark
- Can make rhythmic and consistent marks
- Can make broad and fine marks, depending on the pressure, angle and edge used
- Can be used to 'print' repeatable marks
- Can make interesting textures
- Are efficient at applying water to a chosen area.

Left This bird's-eye view of my table shows some of the huge variety of marks that can be made. Here I've used several sizes of rectangular foam brushes, from 7cm (2¾in) to 2cm (¾in), and every facet of each brush has been used – the tip, wedge, corners and flat sides. In some areas I've applied clean water and run colour into or through that; in others I've made a coloured wash. The surface tension on this calico prevents the water spreading further than the area covered.

Bottom This close-up shows a foam brush calmly at work.

Opposite page

Top Left Here a long woollen scarf is painted using the triangular edge of a foam brush. Each stripe goes across the width of the scarf; no two marks are the same, no two stripes are the same, but the patient application of the marks gives consistency in their effect.

Top Right A scarf painted with the flat sides of the same tool.

Bottom This piece on cotton demonstrates the textured marks that can be made with the flat of the brush, the little triangular corner edges and the fine ridge of the pointed wedge.

Foam Brush Dot Dabbers

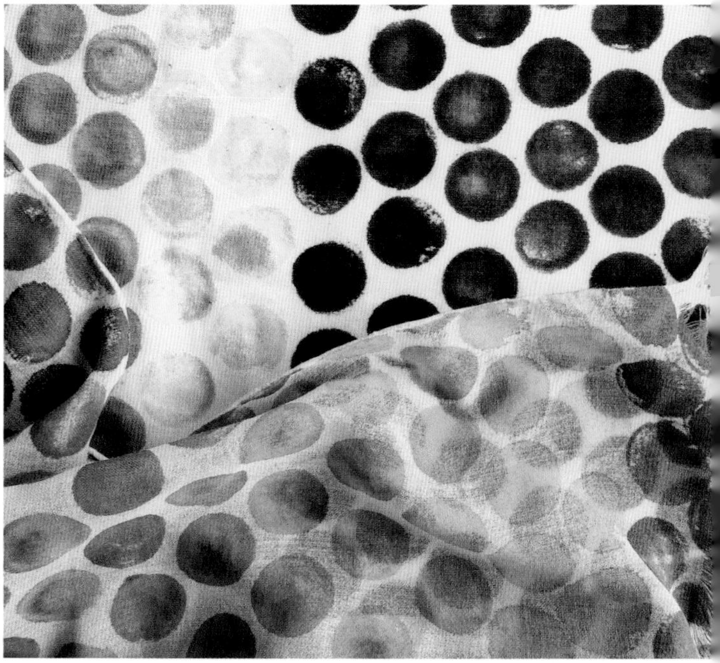

This little mantra of mine – 'one dot does not a pattern make' – serves to remind us that a pattern exists only when multiple marks and motifs come together in whatever relationship the designer dreams up.

Using these dabbers and dobbers is very seductive and moreish – one can really get carried away dotting and spotting all over the place; designs can easily be built up with different colours, sizes and distribution – the perfect illustration of pattern as the accumulation of marks. From large (5cm/2in) to quite little (1.3cm/½in), pressed hard onto the cloth or barely kissing the surface, there's an unending variety of marks to be made. Examples of more uses of these dabbers are dotted throughout the book.

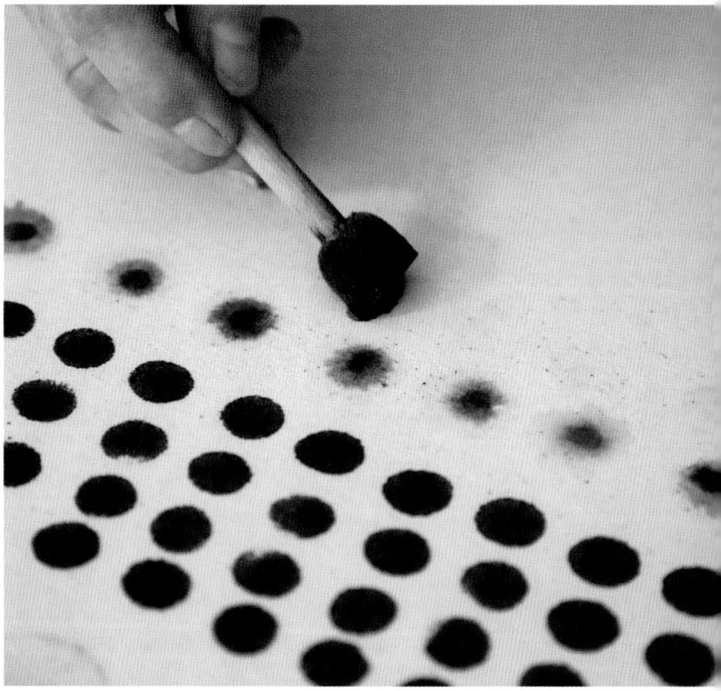

Above Running colour into a clear-water dot.

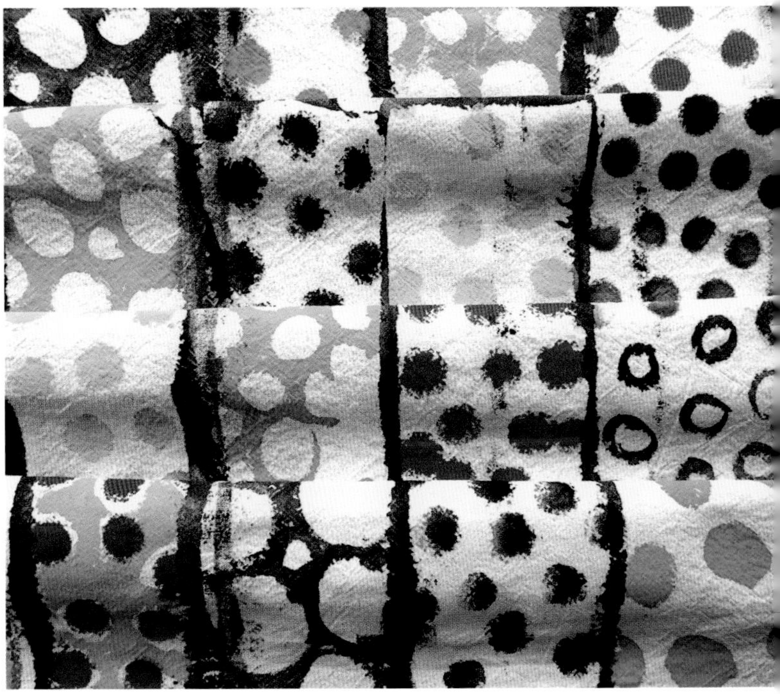

Above Pressing the biggest dabber onto an area of calico dampened with a light-blue wash applied with a wide foam brush.

Left Running colour into a clear-water dot.

Top Right This 'sampler' includes marks made with sponges – man-made, cosmetic and natural, foam dabbers, a pipette, bubble-wrap on the right, and circles made by a loo-roll inner.

Bottom Right Dots in variety made on rough Mexican cotton.

Sponges

Natural and man-made sponges are great ways to make texture. Cosmetic sponges are also some of my favourite handy mark-makers. Available from chemist shops and beauty counters, they come in several standard sizes and shapes.

Above Cosmetic sponges are very dense and can make clear, sharp, repeatable shapes, building up quite a definite and determined pattern.

Above Two sides of the story: this scarf is 'printed' all over with colours applied by the square side of a wedge-shaped cosmetic sponge.

Left Here's a petal-shaped cosmetic sponge on top of marks made with another manufactured sponge that's been soaked in watery paint before being printed.

Bottom Left Natural sea sponges are more expensive and can vary hugely in density, size and quality. They are therefore less predictable in performance. They're great for applying texture and for using with stencils, as we'll see later (see page 90). The soft area in this picture was made using a small sea sponge.

Paintbrushes

The traditional paintbrush allows more expressive marks than a foam brush; being very sensitive to pressure and gesture, it can really be an extension of one's hand. There are many sorts of brushes with special names, particular uses and histories developed over centuries. They are made from various hairs, bristles, whiskers, filaments and fibres which have been designed to offer the best exploitation and application of the various artists' paint mediums, with longer and shorter handles, and wider and narrower heads to make them more efficient and effective in their wielding. Here I am just going to talk about the two most generally available shapes: the square flat end and the round pointable end, but it's fun and fascinating to experiment with a whole range of brushes.

Sketchbook painting of the brush wall at the Stuart R. Stevenson shop in London.

Flat-ended Paintbrushes

Top This bird's-eye view shows some of the marks that can be made using flat-ended brushes.

Left A twirling, twisting stroke with the flat brush can give the appearance of a swirling ribbon.

Top A shorter-handled, broader flat-ended brush can make a lyrical dash, a quick flick, with an emphatic pressure on the downward stroke.

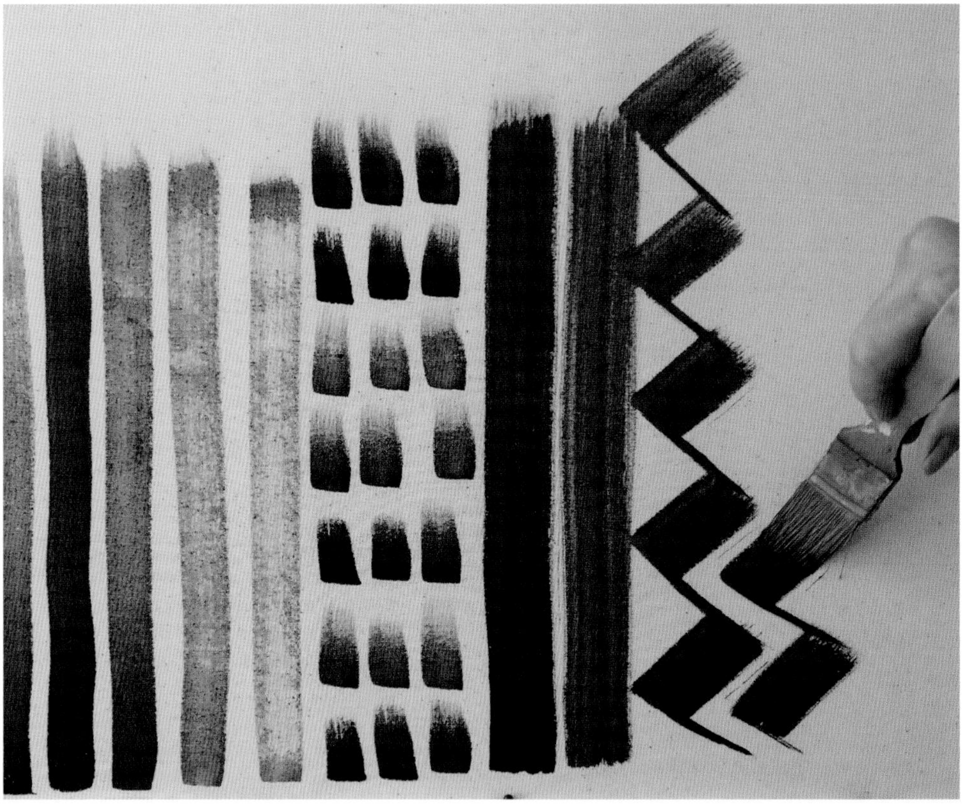

Above Here you can see the very reliable build-up of marks achieved by applying consistent and repetitive pressure. To make these sorts of patterns, it helps to get into a rhythm where you can get attuned to the action and really feel the actual time it takes to make the mark – simple changes of colour and brush size can bring variety.

Top This pattern is built upon a simple layout of rectangles, giving a nod to the idea of horizontal and vertical blocks in a weave. These marks are all made with the same flat-ended 1.5cm (5/8in) brush. When the marks were dry, I ran over them with red and yellow inks to add liveliness and a unifying theme. Painted on a natural linen, nothing was measured or ruled – the irregularities and wobbles added liveliness, and my guess is that the size of the blocks was dictated by how much paint that particular brush held in one stroke.

Left I'm giving this brush full pressure all the way along the stroke to squeeze every bit of yellow out of it!

Bottom Left Different marks need different widths and types of flat brushes and, depending on the mark required, these are held and used in different ways. Good balance, with feet firmly on the ground if standing, makes for a steady hand; here I'm using my little finger to give my painting action more control. To make the different marks with conviction, it's good to be flexible in holding and moving the brush in order to feel its power and delivery.

Round Paintbrushes

Paintbrushes with fine tips are the most pliable of all the tools I've described so far. A good brush with a fine point that holds paint well gives the opportunity for real expression and drawing in your work.

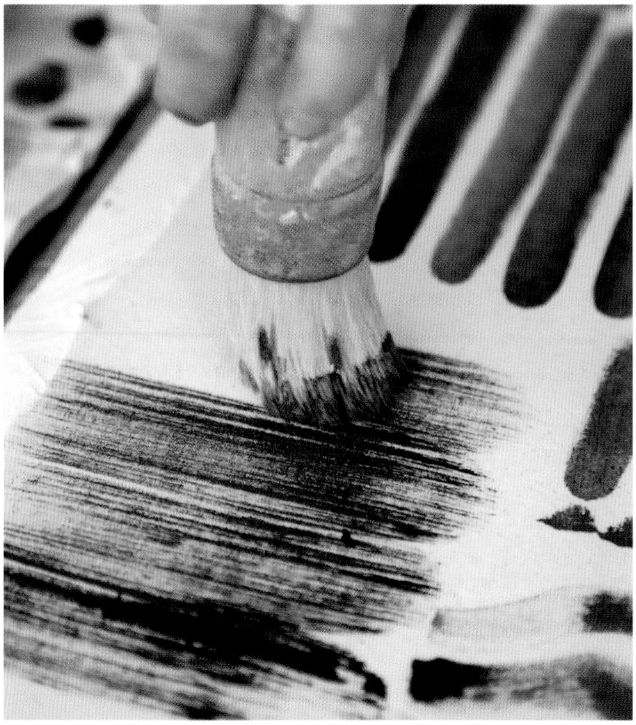

Top Left Here I'm using a large number 12 brush with man-made bristles – a very satisfactory, versatile tool! The marks in the first row of waving lines – made by pressing hard for the full down stroke and lifting off for the fine one – made me think of birds. I was able make them with one simple stroke and then add a feather crest and stick legs with the very tip of the brush.

Above Huge brush.

Bottom Left The same brush, pressed down partway onto the cloth from the tip in a rhythmic motion.

Opposite page
Top Left Tiny brush.

Top Right Little circles, watery circles, flowery circles.

Bottom Several brushes, and what they can do.

PAINTING INTO WATER

There are some times when water dropped on cloth is an absolute nuisance and others when it's part of a deliberate strategy. In the case of the former, mop the water up with kitchen towel or a clean rag as quickly and carefully as you can and dry the patch with a hairdryer. In the case of the latter, learning to control the water is key. One good way is with a little pipette, or even your clean-water squeezy bottle, but often the droplets can take a while to dry.

Above Here I've made some little water blobs with a dropper and I'm running colour in from the same small pipette.

Right I like to run water across cloth using a foam brush and then seep paint into the wetness. These circles were made this way, and you can see the surface tension (or meniscus) as the colour disperses into the wet area and sits tight on the dry.

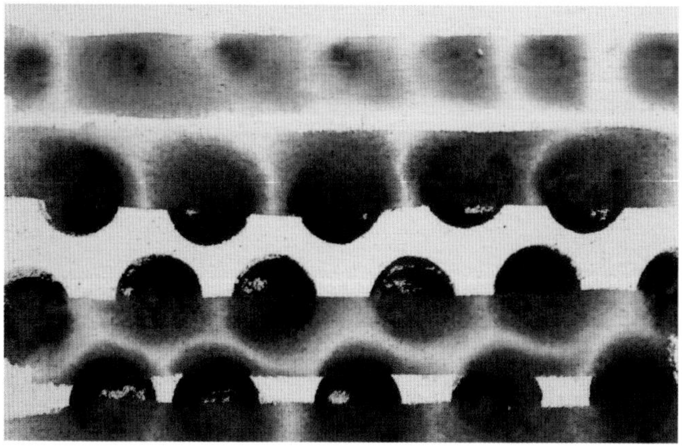

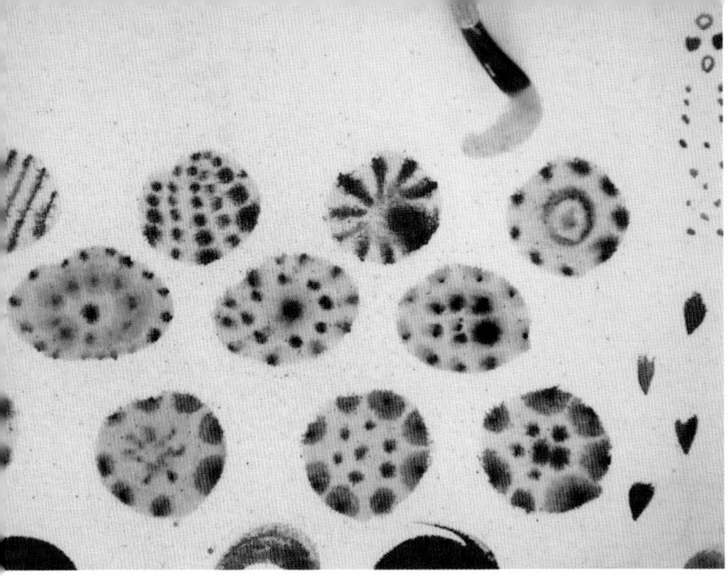

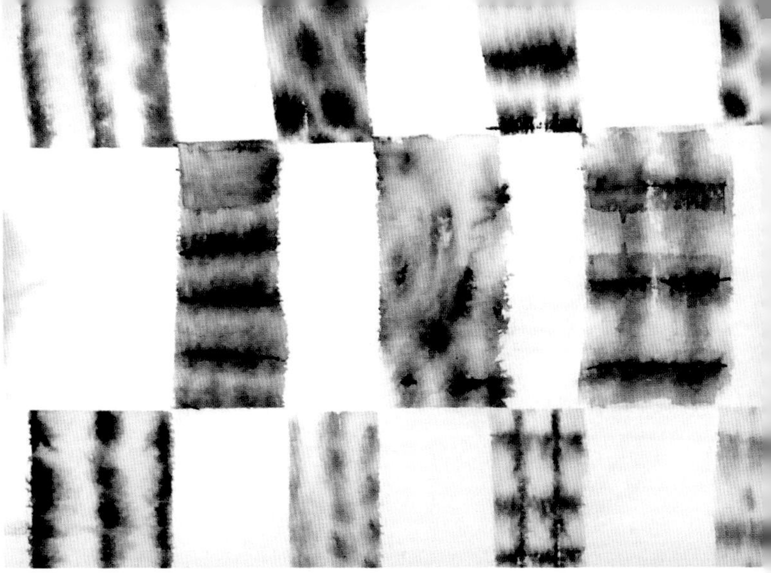

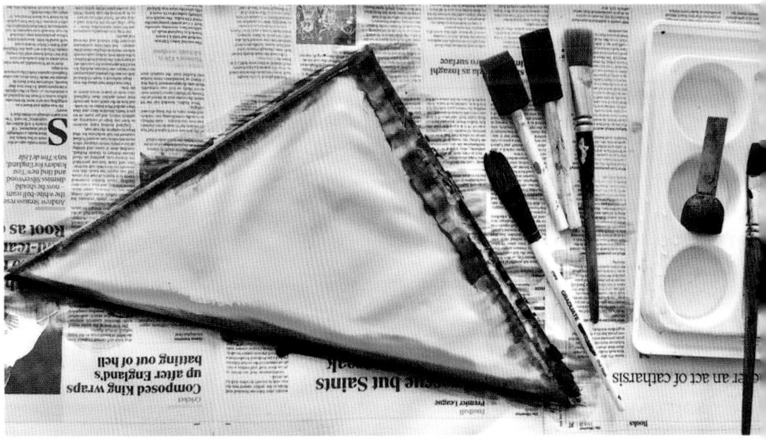

If you pin your cloth to a plastic-covered foam board, the water will sit longer and the colour remains strong. If you're painting on a fabric backing, the colour can seep away into it, leaving a pale effect on your fabric.

Above These clear-water circles are made with a foam brush dabber. I've run tiny specks of colour into them using a small pointed brush. They have a look of Murano millefiori glass; the water sits on the cloth and the colours migrate only as far as the water's edge.

Top Right Here I'm painting into a chequerboard of clear water. Again, the colour disperses only as far as the water extends.

Middle Right A close look at the effect of painting dry paint over wet and letting it go where it will.

Bottom Right Folding the cloth and then seeping water and paint into the folds makes a very nice pleated effect (see page 120).

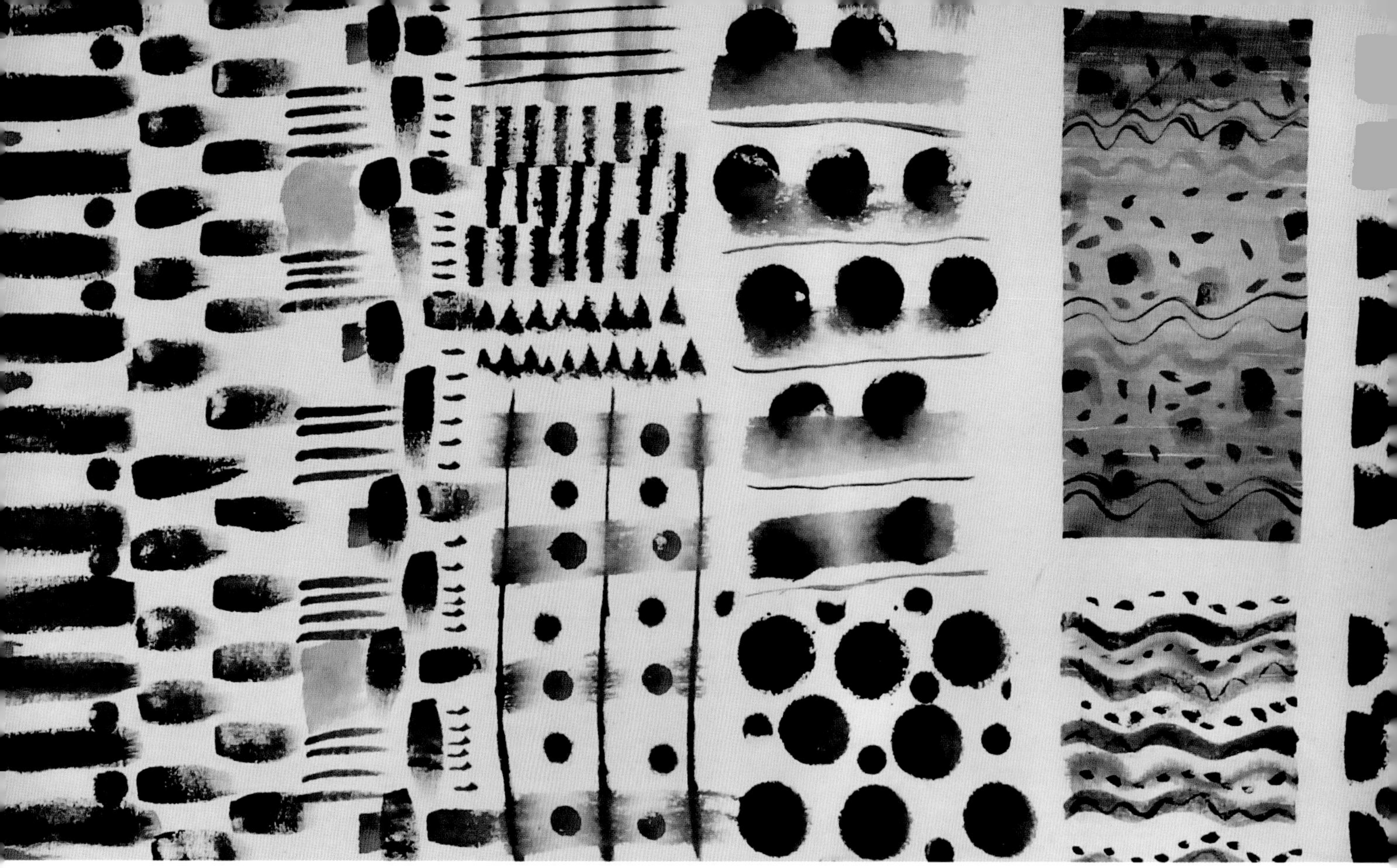

Chapter One

MAKING A START WITH MAKING A MARK

Having now seen what some of these tools can do, for your first project you could make yourself a sampler, either as a reference piece or to be made into a bag or a cushion. Start by stretching and pinning a piece of fabric (a 30cm/12in strip of calico will do) flat onto your board or table, putting some paint into a palette and choosing some brushes or sponges.

Starting with just one colour (I favour black for this work) take time to experience the pulse of making marks, from that familiar heartbeat to more elaborate rhythms, working down and across the cloth, recording the actions of your hand and the brush. It'll take a bit of experimenting to get your paint to the consistency you want as there are many variables at play: cloth, atmosphere, paint, brushes, pressure – these all affect how things work, so be patient and curious in equal measure.

Give yourself the experience of building up areas of different rhythmic marks. Sometimes it can help to make these marks to a beat, an interval or a count – one long stroke, two short, for instance; one hefty dot followed by a little dab, rather like a morse code message. You can attune to how long it takes to make different marks. This way of making marks freely, just for the experience, can loosen up the muscles and banish some of the preconceptions and judgements that get in the way of discovery. It's not about how it looks, but more about how it feels. I often do this exercise with my eyes shut.

Below When teaching a longer course, the students and I begin by taking an exploratory journey painting on rolls of lining paper. This picture was taken at the end of a first day (of three).

As a next step, with the idea of making more deliberate decisions, it can be useful to divide the fabric's surface into sections using masking or decorator's tape. This will help you to see each painted area clearly – your marks can be well-contained and easily read within these smaller sections. Defining the areas of pattern, painting right up to and over the edges of the tape, also gives you the chance to make quite flowing, expressive gestures: they don't have to stop short or be curtailed, so even if the entirety cannot be seen, its nature can be understood.

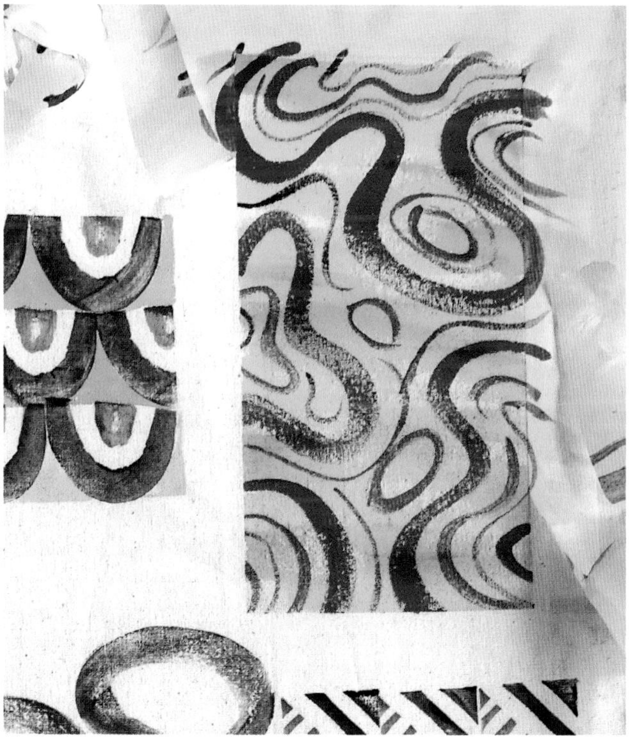

Above One student told me that at this stage she thought of her piece of fabric as a garden and she was marking out her seed beds with the tape – a useful analogy.

Experiment with the tools you have to hand and with the different viscosities of your paint and ink, from dry to watery, and build up a language of marks. These can change as you go along, but keeping them within the boundaries of the tape helps you to see the pattern's intention, making it easier to evaluate. Your eye can take in an area of contained pattern, however small (think of patchwork), whereas it is more difficult to read the effect of an area with undefined edges.

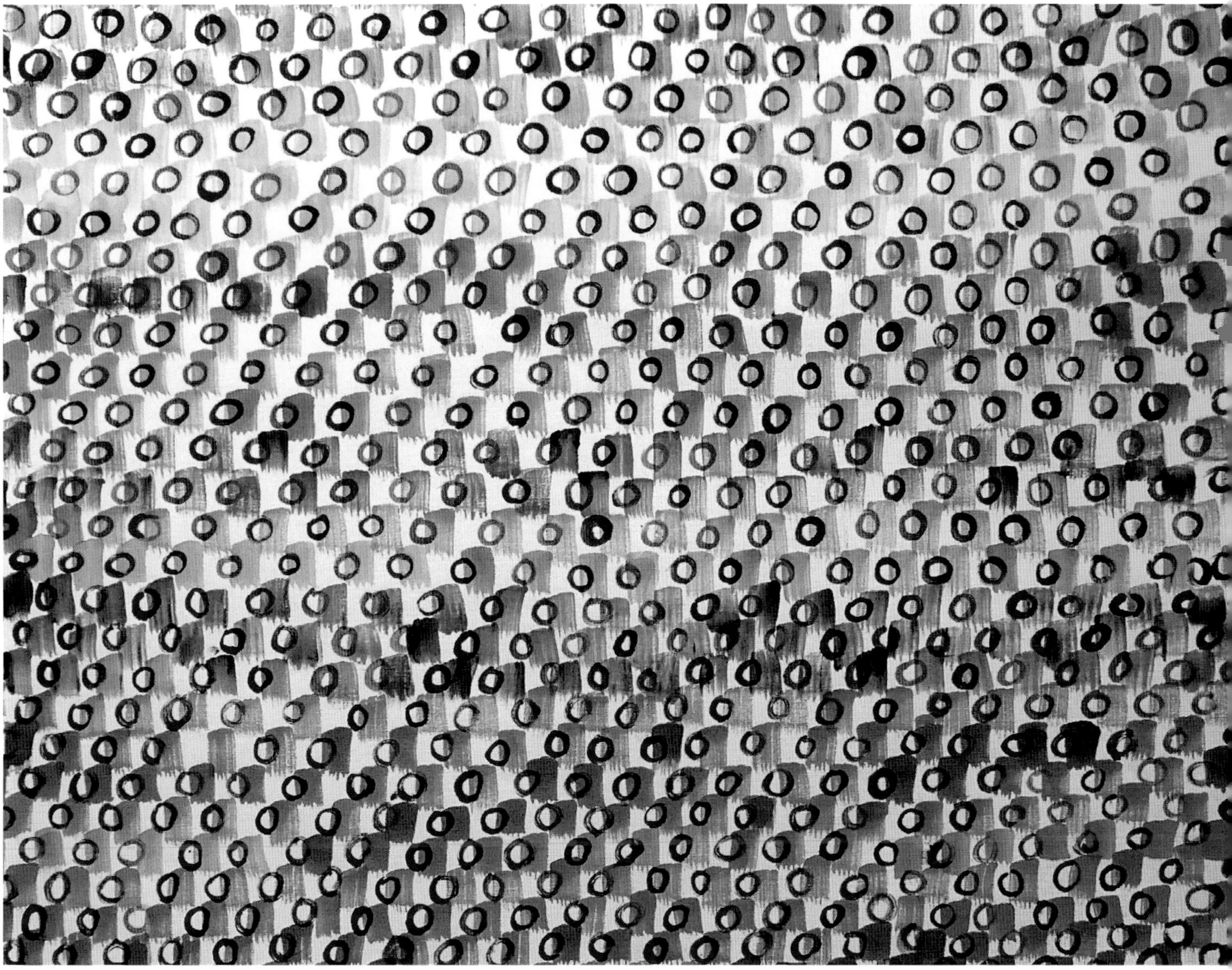

Once the piece has dried – which can be hastened with a hairdryer – other colours can be run in and painted on to give different emphases and depths to the marks. If you're planning to make a bag or a cushion, remember they have two sides – giving two opportunities for a series of experiments. Try using only black paint on one side and black with colour on the other, for instance, or a series of stripes and then a series of spots, or a dramatic change of scale. It's rewarding to really work through your ideas: small changes and progressions can make quite a large impact.

Project
PAINTING A READY-MADE BAG

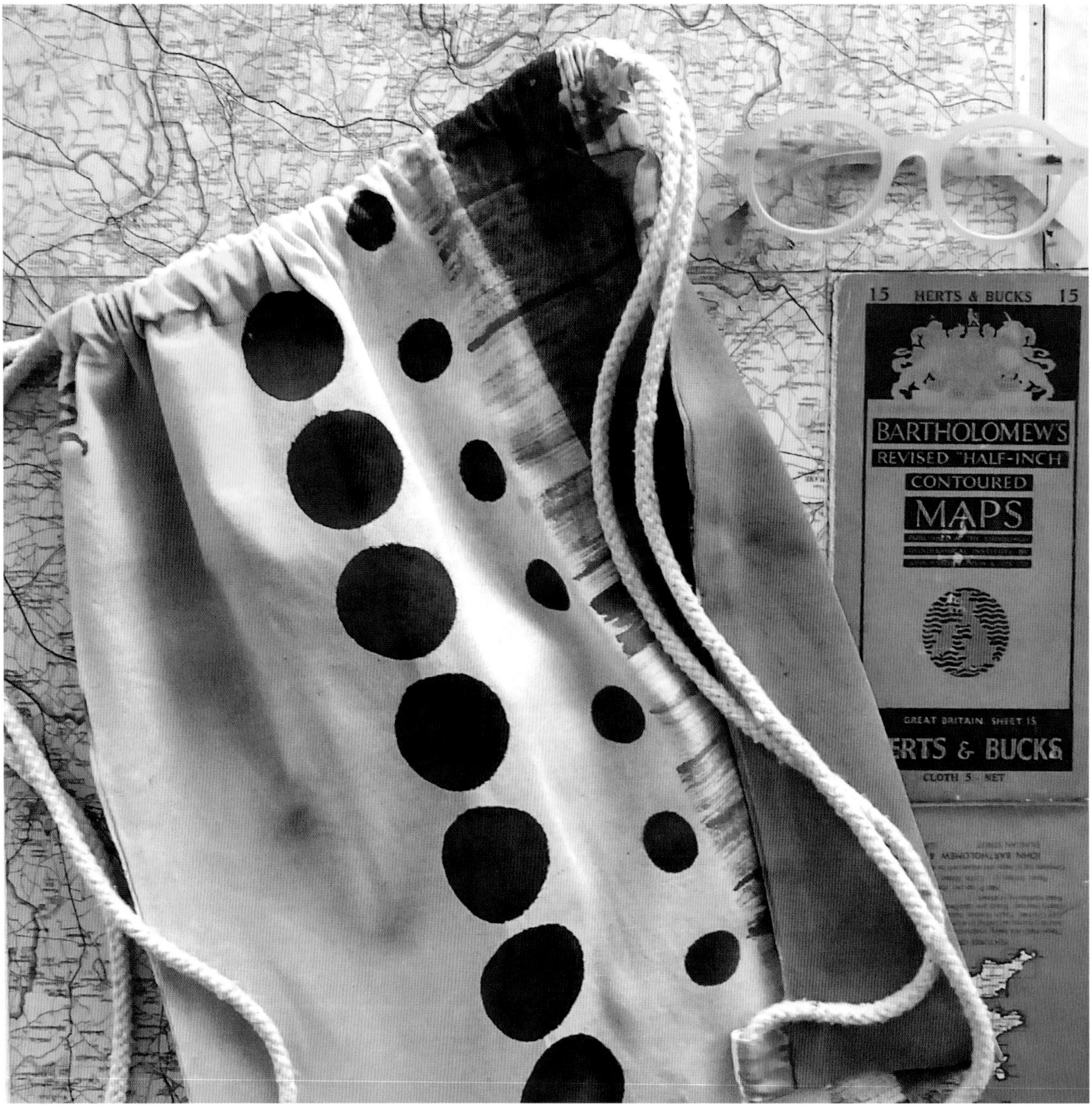

Ready-made calico and canvas totes, bags and accessories are widely available if sewing isn't your... 'bag'! But they're simple to make yourself too. For this project I chose a ready-made cotton drawstring bag that can be worn on the back or over one shoulder as a duffel bag. I was careful not to paint the cords. I had the design for the front and back in mind from the start – mainly orange one side and yellow the other, but both sharing secondary colours – quite a limited palette.

One of the facts of life when it comes to fabric painting is that it's impossible to get a really large, flat, consistent wash of colour. The moment you apply the ink or paint, it starts to sink into the cloth and dry. Luckily, our eyes don't worry about this too much and we tend to read an area of one colour as flat, but look carefully and you will discern tonality – variations in colour tone and depth.

On the other hand, the great advantage of making an area of colour (tonal or not) is that when dry, it gives a fine surface layer to the cloth – this acts as a barrier or skin upon which you can paint and draw without fear of the ink running into the warp and weft of the open cloth.

This piece shows fine lines drawn on a coloured ground.

There are a couple of large areas of single colours – the orange and the yellow – painted on the little bag opposite to demonstrate the 'flat/not flat' effect. It's also a good example of simple mark making using a couple of different tools – dabbers, brushes and tape – with the idea of making consistent but different designs on front and back.

You Will Need

- Pencils
- Paper
- Auto-fade pen
- Fabric paints/inks
- Iron
- Ready-made cotton drawstring bag
- Paper to line the bag
- A board or surface on which to pin the bag
- Pushpins or map pins
- Masking tape or Tesa tape
- Hairdryer (optional)
- Brushes: foam and bristle

Method

1 You might like to draw a plan of your design before you start, remembering that the back and the front offer the opportunity for difference – complement or contrast, it's up to you. If you want to draw on the fabric itself, be sure to use an auto-fade pen.

2 Plan and prepare your colours in a palette or small containers. They could be similar to the bag shown here or adapted to your taste, remembering that when painting one colour over another you need dark to go over light to read well.

3 Iron the bag and line it with paper so that the paint doesn't leak through from one side to the other.

4 Pin the bag flat to the board. You are now ready to paint the first area of colour (for me, the orange) with a wide brush.

5 Run tape down the bag to give the colour a sharp, neat edge. I find this bag itself such a tidy little rectangle that I want my design to complement it.

6 When the paint is dry (hairdryer to the ready!), lift the tape and place it in a different position to give another neat edge to paint against. This time make blue textured horizontal stripes with a narrower flat brush. Each time, the size and shape of the brush is integral to the marks being made.

7 On the other side, repeat a similar process (using different proportions) for the yellow area. This side is a little more elaborate. Use a large foam dabber for the blue dots – I like them landing half and half.

8 To echo the front, paint another rust-coloured band and run blue textured stripes across it, again using the narrow bristle brush. Add smaller rust-coloured dots to dance down the bag.

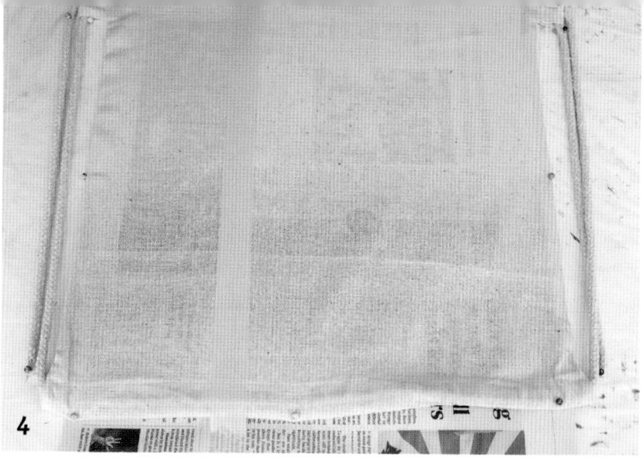

4

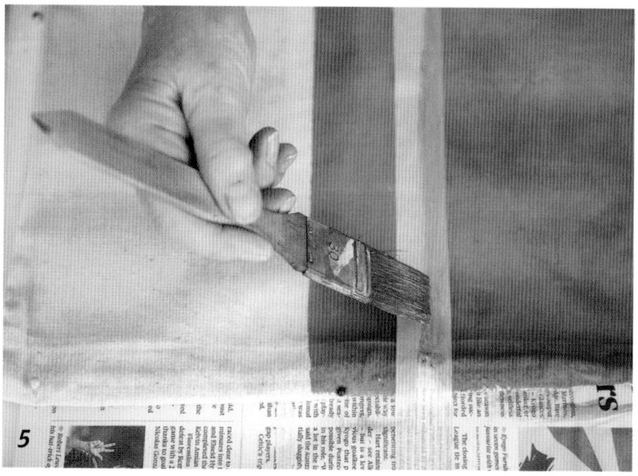

5

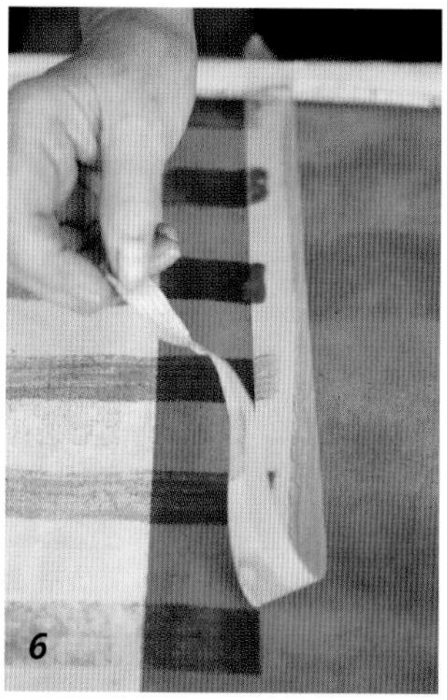

6

7

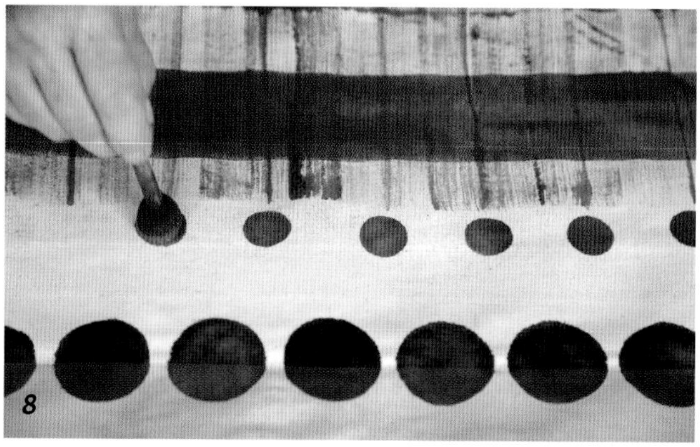

8

9 The last detail is to paint the little tabs that hold the cord: blue one side, rust the other.

Below The pattern on this bag is an uncomplicated and clear design; nevertheless the balance between colour and mark is crucial in even the simplest of patterns.

CARRYALL AND PICNIC MAT ALL-IN-ONE

This larger bag is one of my home-made inventions, designed in this case to double up as an outdoor sit-upon mat. I don't sew the front and back together on this bag, and I leave the sides open so I can slip two pieces of yoga mat or similar inside – when opened out I'll be more comfortable sitting on the grass. All will become clear as we progress... Other uses are available!

The mat has a very basic shape and uses simple wide-width calico, which is usually around 1.3m (51in) wide. I divide the calico, cutting 50cm (20in) for the front and 50cm (20in) for the inside, and use the remainder for handles and pockets.

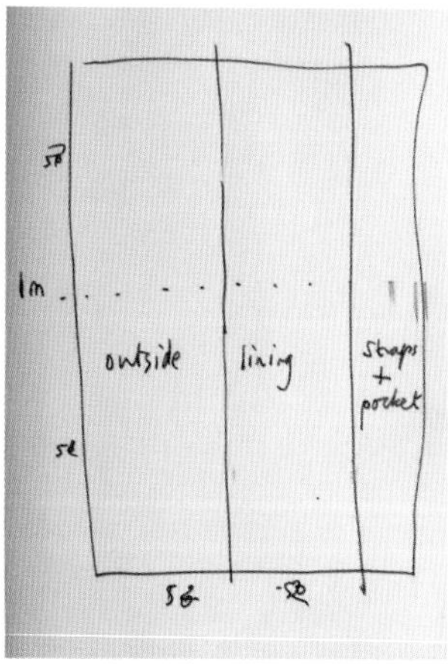

Above My little drawing is more of a map or a diagram of how to apportion the fabric.

Right I started with both a colour and a mark strategy planned out for this design. I decided to make a colour division: blues on one half of the cloth and multicolours on the other. This way, the bag will be versatile and look good worn with denim, black, white and all stops in between. I also planned to use two sorts of mark-making tools: paintbrushes for the more rectangular marks on the outside, and round dabbers and dotters to make circles and dots for the inside and flat foam.

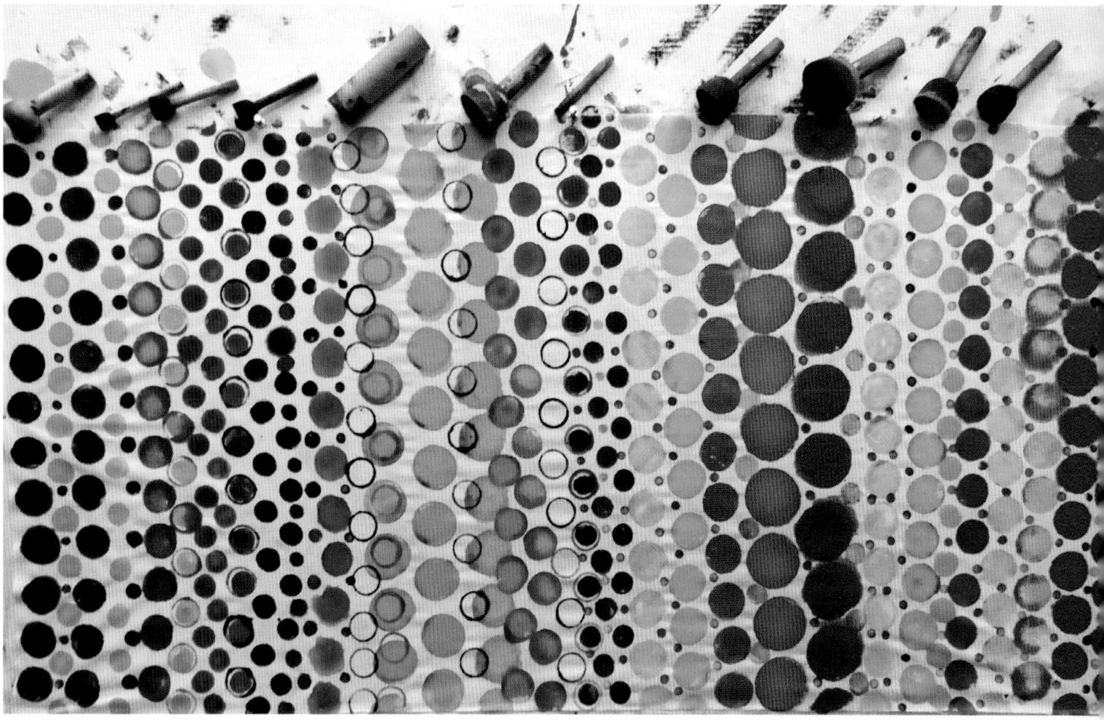

Overleaf These are the three pieces when painted.

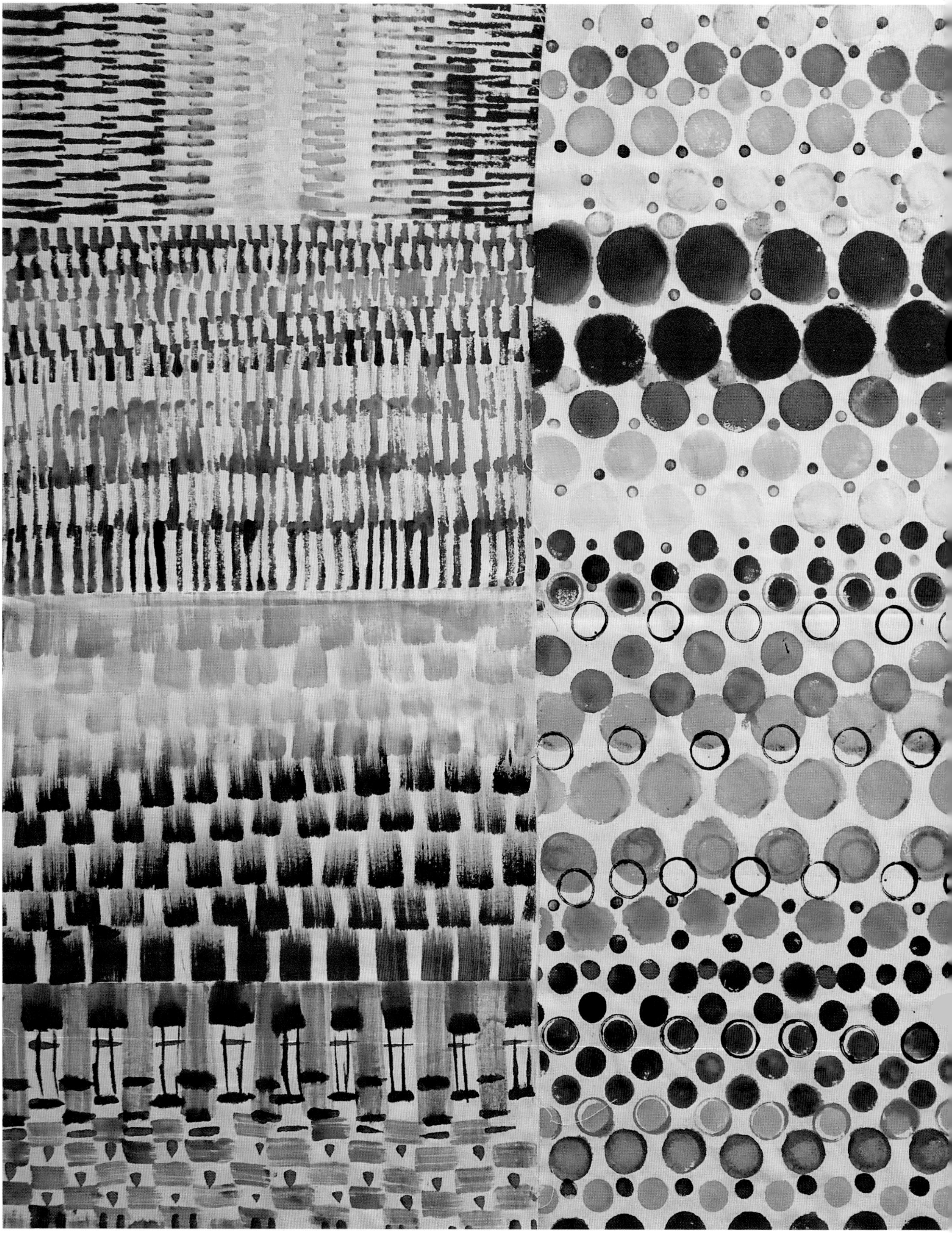

Left The pockets, lining and straps all have the same half-and-half colour division, giving the opportunity for playing with juxtaposing colours.

I needed to mix a good amount of paint in my palettes, though I almost always adapt and vary colours within the range on a tray as I go along.

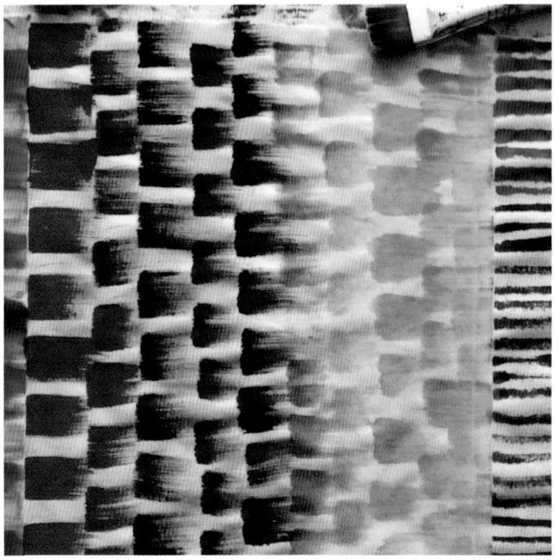

Far Left A closer look at the outside, how the marks have been made using a variety of brushes and techniques, masking off areas where necessary and building up the collection of blues.

Left Here, the brush marks build up the colour and pattern on a pocket area.

THIS LARGER BAG IS ONE OF MY HOME-MADE INVENTIONS, DESIGNED IN THIS CASE TO DOUBLE UP AS AN OUTDOOR SIT-UPON MAT

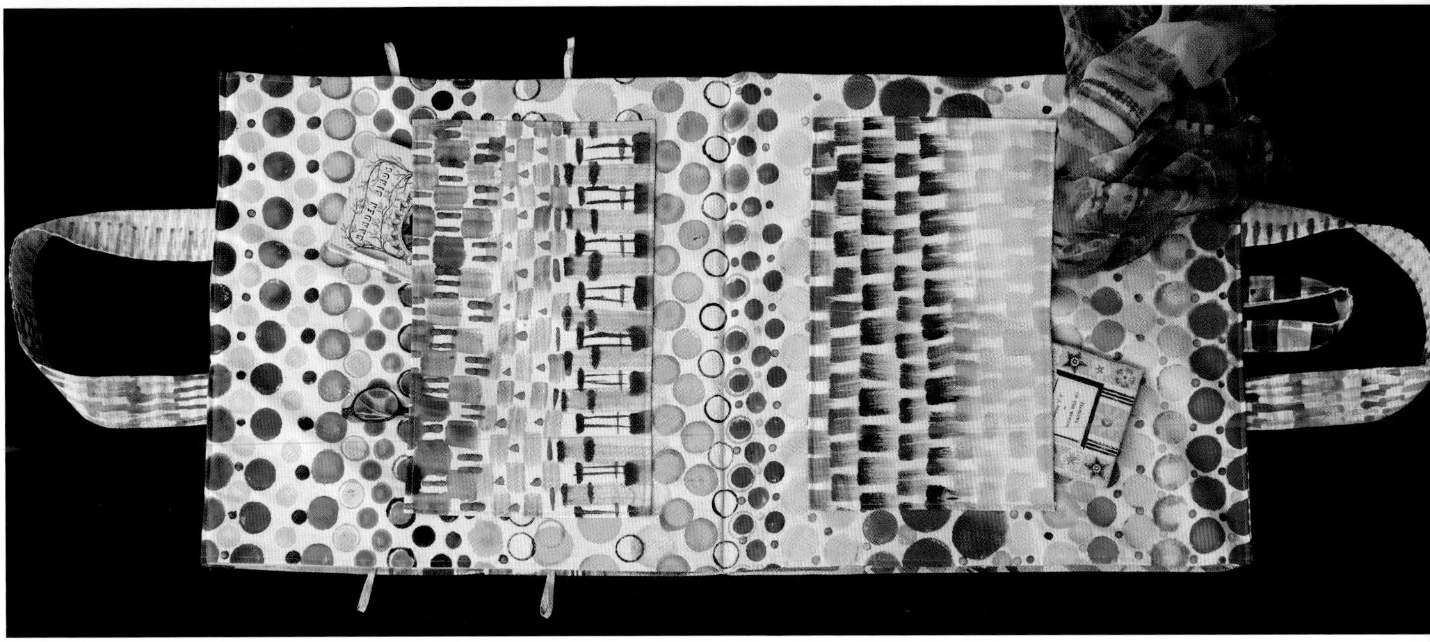

Top The front and back are sewn together as a flat piece, inserting the top carrying handles and the side closure button loops in the seams.

Middle and Right Two 'slices' of mat or foam can be cut to fit and slipped into the open-sided sections, so when folded to be carried as a bag, a book and a sandwich can be popped into the pockets. Upon arrival, the whole thing can be opened out as quite a good-sized sit-upon for a grassy relax.

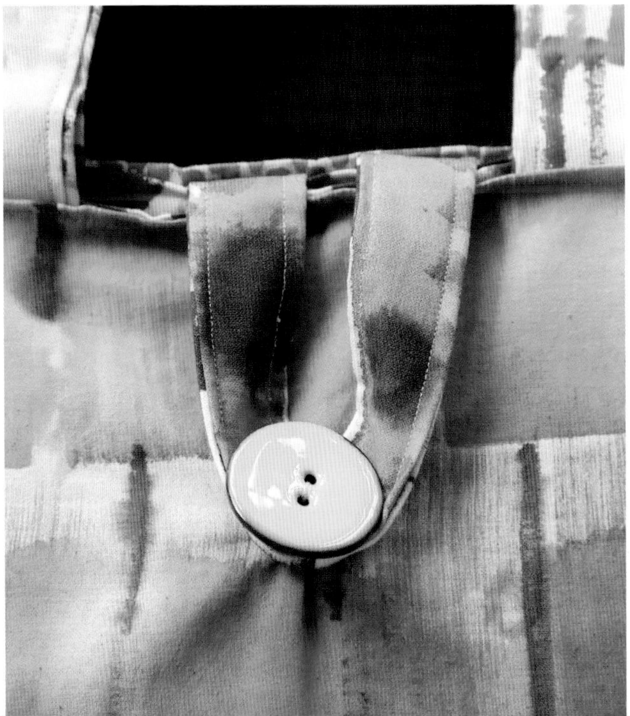

Three Potatoes, oil on brown paper, by Tony Beaver.

Chapter Two POTATOES

One of the simplest, most direct and versatile ways of hand-painting pattern onto cloth is via the potato. Many people remember making potato prints as children and are often astounded at how versatile, effective and rewarding they can be. As one surprised adult said when I proposed this method, 'What, you mean a *real* potato?'

During the long loneliness of the first pandemic lockdown in 2020, I enjoyed quite a few potato-printing and painting days at home, and wrote this little rhyme to celebrate:

the tatty, spud or murphy,
kartoshka, purdie, knish,
can be mashed or boiled or roasted
or baked within a dish;
but prime amongst its uses,
through all these darkest days,
when cut and carved and painted
we can print it – many ways.

The potato – cut, carved and coloured – gives a quickly repeatable motif, with the rhythm and spacing easily controllable, either by eye or with a simple measure. It is a brilliant example of making pattern by accumulation.

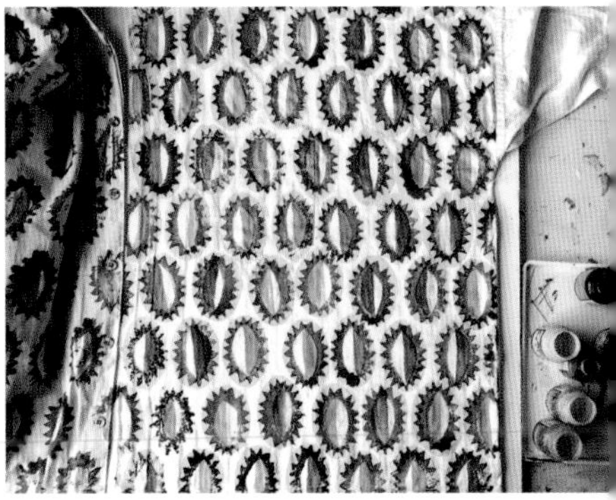

Above This must be the simplest potato print ever! It was made using a quartered potato on a T-shirt. No design was cut; I used the shape simply as a consistent vehicle to carry colour. The interest is achieved by the changes in colour tones – the potato was painted anew between each print down – and the density and persistence of the application. In places, I've also added to the pattern with painted marks. I did this as a workshop demonstration and one student asked me could I turn some of the marks into leaves, so I did!

Top Right Mixing techniques, simple printing and painting gives the possibility of making an interesting repeating pattern, full of movement and variety. I'd made a very simple cut using the natural shape of a halved potato as a demonstration on a short course I was teaching. The print became a face, then became a stripe, then became a very fetching little piece of linen. It's a scrap of fabric, 30cm (12in) square or so, that always gets a smile and a positive reaction.

Middle Right I decided a much-loved old cotton shirt of mine could do with perking up, so I reached for a potato!

Bottom Right On this piece, the only part printed is the repeating oval surrounding the faces. The other parts have been hand-painted in afterwards – quite untidily, in fact. The potato placement was not measured – I trusted to my instinct and experience; so, though variable, the rhythm of the marks carries the pattern.

Main image To cover such a lot of fabric, one needs a certain amount of patience and persistence – one may almost say obsession! To keep myself entertained, when it came to the back of the shirt, I continued with the same shape but printed it down in a different configuration – horizontally instead of running north-south.

Below The final fun was writing on the sleeve, 'If the sun and moon should doubt. They'd immediately go out' from William Blake's 'Auguries of Innocence' – a favourite of mine. When I started on this piece I had no idea how it would end up.

Process
MAKING A POTATO PRINT

You Will Need

- Potatoes
- Sharp chef's knife (large and small)
- Cutting board or mat
- Pen
- Scalpel and/or lino-cutting tools
- Fabric paints/inks
- Paintbrushes
- Fabric to print
- A board or surface on which to pin it
- Kitchen towel

Method

1 Slice your potatoes. Remember there is more than one way to make the slice – across and along, width, length and height – like measuring a parcel for UPS! Your first cut needs to be as straight and determined as possible – that will be your printing face. I use a good sharp chef's knife for this.

2 It can be useful to draw the motif out before you begin to cut your design.

3 Use a smaller chef's knife, a sharp scalpel and/or lino-cutting tools to make gouges, channels and dots in the cut potato.

4 You can vary the colours on a cut as you progress. I often paint more than one colour at the same time to give depth and variety to my designs. I try to use a different brush for each colour to keep the paint clean.

5 Add final details with a paintbrush to give the print extra definition, if desired.

Project
MAKING A PORTABLE GAMES BOARD

Here's how to make a fabric chess or draughts board using a potato print with hand-painted borders. The size is up to you, with the proviso that the playing area needs to be square and must accommodate sixty-four alternately coloured squares inside: eight across and eight down (I tend to make mine 4cm (1½in) square). You could sew a backing to this cloth and add a drawstring to make it into a bag in which to stash the playing pieces.

You Will Need

- Square of calico (a finished size of about 40cm/16in square gives a good playing area with space for the decorative borders)
- Board or surface on which to pin or tape your cloth
- Pushpins or map pins
- Ruler or tape measure
- Masking tape (I use Tesa tape)
- Potato
- Cutting board or mat
- Sharp chef's knife
- Scalpel and lino-cutting tools (optional)
- Fabric paints/inks
- Paintbrushes
- Pencil and/or auto-fade pen
- Kitchen towel or rag

Tip

Having cut my square of calico, I often sew the hem before printing so I know where I am.

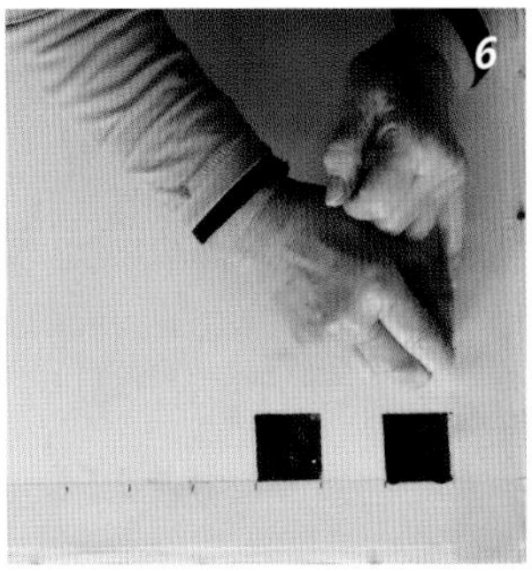

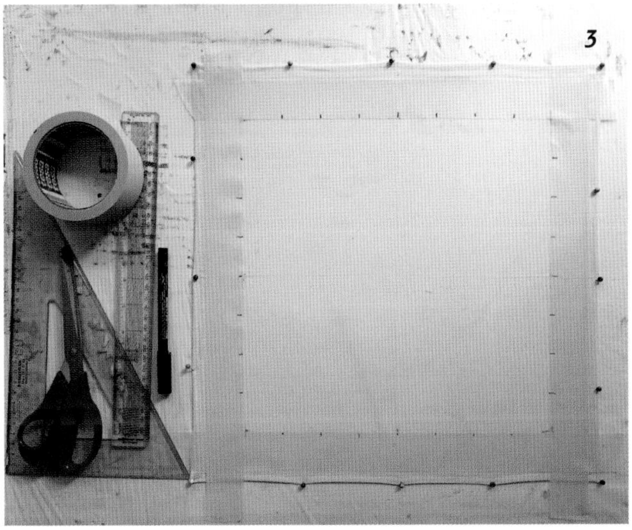

Method

1 Find and mark the centre of the cloth – a simple fold into quarters will guide you. Calculated from the centre, the playing squares can then run equidistantly towards the edges.

2 Pin the fabric flat on the board, stretching it as you go to make a smooth surface upon which to work.

3 On the cloth, make a frame with masking tape to enclose the area of the chequerboard print. Mark the intervals to show where to place your potato. I marked onto the tape with a pencil.

4 Cut your potato into a square, according to your chosen measurements (this one is 4cm/1½in square). I find it helpful to make a little square paper template as a cutting guide.

5 Paint the potato's printing surface. I use a paintbrush and traditional black paint for this.

6 Place the potato down carefully into a taped corner and apply even pressure with your hand. Try not to wiggle it! Lift the potato off cleanly.

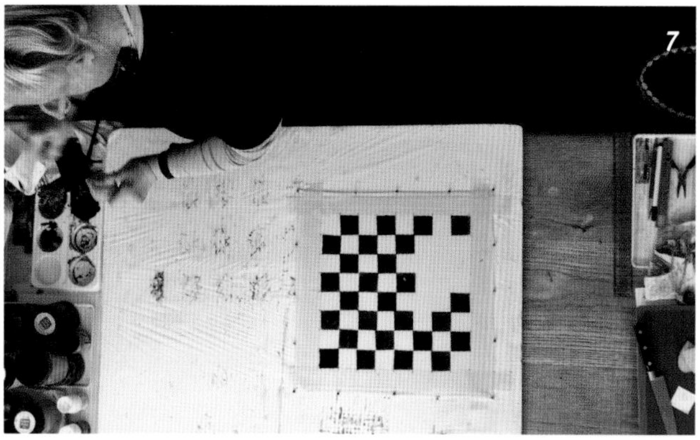

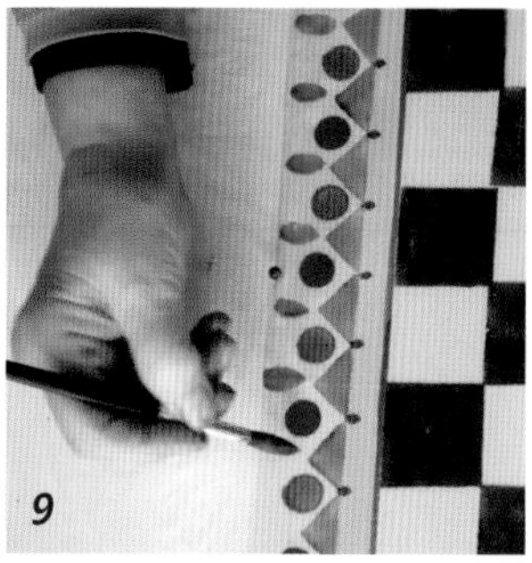

Tip

If you're nervous about the squares joining up, you could draw the grid out with an auto-fade pen before you start.

7 Work your way along one edge of the tape and then along the perpendicular edge. You then have the framework in which to print across the piece, matching the corners of the potato each time. You may get a little wobble here and there, but I think that adds to the charm.

8 When the centre is complete, lift the tape. Now it's time to think about painting the borders. You can mask off the central area so your border is neat – simply run the tape over the chequerboard when it's dry.

9 Add the finishing touches to the border.

Above If this is destined as a gift, you could incorporate a name and/or favourite colours at this point. I recently painted a board for someone who loves clouds, so the cloth got a heavenly border – the chess pieces looked as though they were floating in the sky!

MORE POTATOES!

Pattern accumulates, as I've said more than once, and potato prints lend themselves beautifully to this process.

A Grainy Potato

This pattern of ovals was created by simply painting a band around the cut edge of a potato half and printing it down! I then cut the terracotta-coloured centre shape and printed down the whole thing like that. The potato was a little grainy and the print purchase wasn't good, so I painted in the missing middle parts with yellow. After some thought, I painted in the black background. Then I cut the potato in half and turned it into the fish scales pattern above; or seen the other way up and coloured differently, they could become rainbows!

Geometric Patterns

Different patterns can be built up, depending on how you place and colour the spud – changes of orientation and colour distribution can give many variations. In any event, the colour needs to be freshly applied between each print down. The potato can be washed and wiped dry when colours need changing. Using two or even three colours on one potato requires a little care, but I find the results compelling and the variety of patterns quite mesmerising.

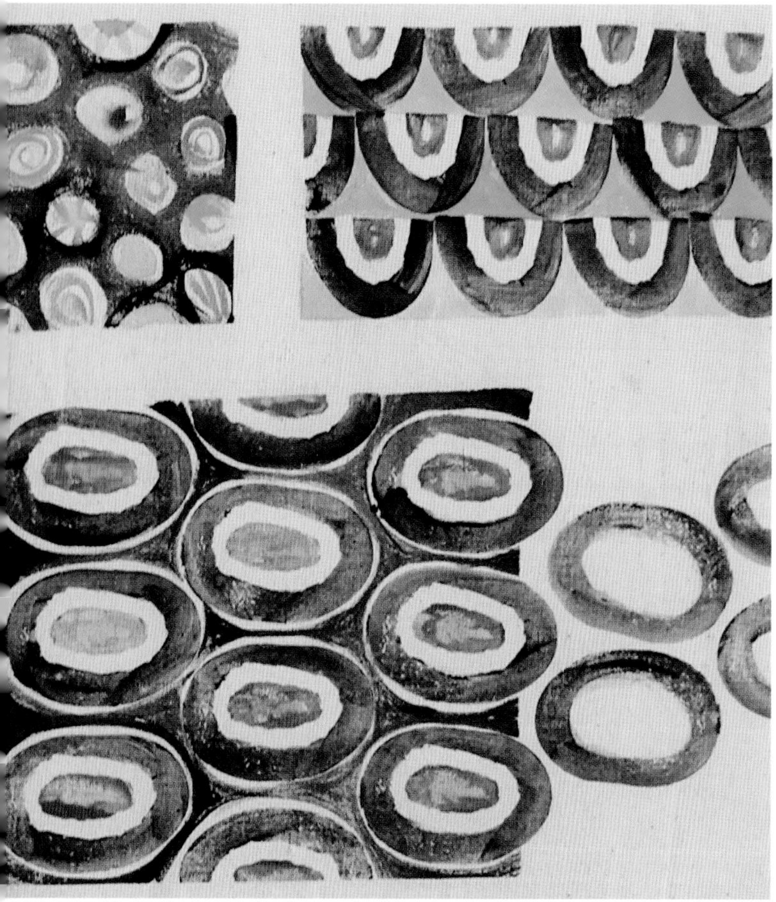

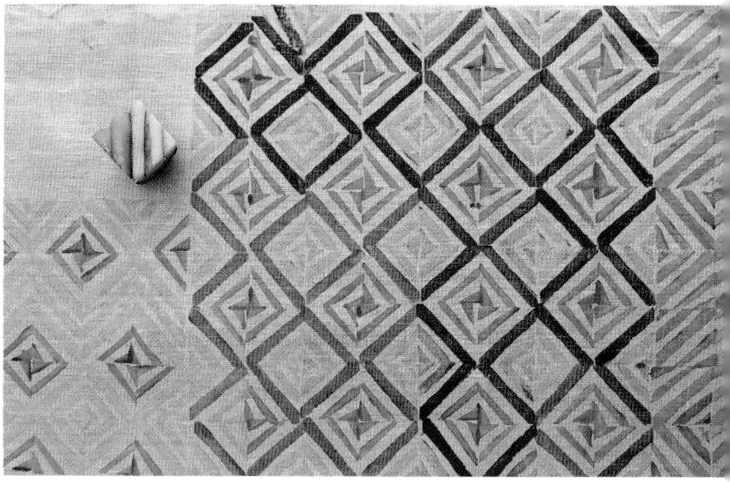

Several applications of the same cut pattern, printed on a natural linen.

Left A simple geometric potato print can quickly build up into an interesting field of tessellated, overlapped or adjacent patterns. I like to cut the potato into a rectangle or square for this, and then cut a simple set of lines: diagonal or straight.

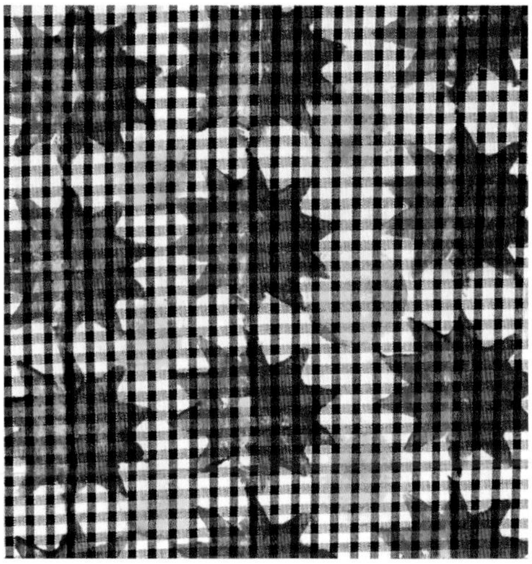

Left In this pattern, the unit of potato is a small simple half-star. How it's placed and coloured makes such a difference to the outcome. Here on the left of the fabric it's twisted and turned; on the right it's matched and mirrored with another colour. Both patterns have a dabbed-on dot to give focus. Here it is again, on the right, printed down on a little gingham check. This picture shows a scrap of how things can develop – clearly some ideas work better than others!

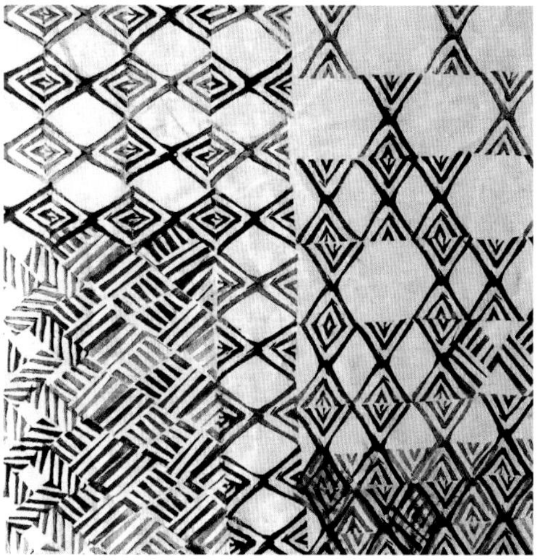

Bottom This cut – two linear triangles on one potato – offers a lot of variation. Printed here on linen, it's nice just in simple black, and intriguing as it builds.

Flowers and Leaves

It could be that a leaf or flower shape seems more of a traditional motif for a potato cut, reflecting as it does the natural shape of the tuber.

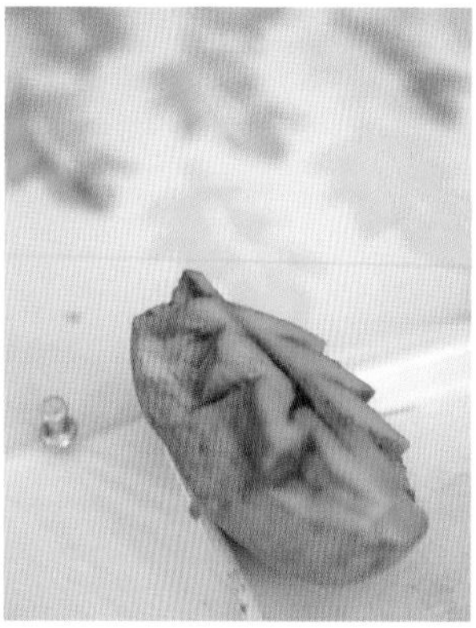

Above Here are several different leaves put down in a variety of ways with painted lines, dots or motifs added later – a field of pattern, a vine, a border.

Below This type of flower is also a very simple and typical print, made more interesting by using three colours on each print: pink, red and a green stalk.

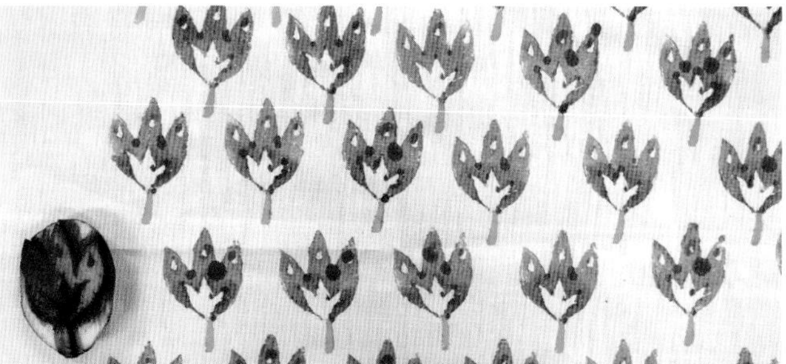

Top This is the same cut, printed on a deeper-coloured ground cloth, using earthy tones to make a different colourway.

Above With other printed and painted details added, that pink flower developed into a panel...

Above ...And here it is made up into a cushion.

Blackbirds and a Pond

My sister had a shallow pond in her garden where the birds loved to wash and splash, and she really enjoyed watching them at play. They were the inspiration for this little cushion.

I used the two halves of a big potato to cut the two birds: one potato simply sliced to make the oval pond and the other cut into bits and pieces for the little growing flowers and reeds. Having printed down the pond and the birds, I then painted a pink background, leaving the blackbird scene as a cameo.

The piece with the blue background is a little different, using one repeating bird, no pond and some patterns painted in the background (maybe I did this piece first and got a little more ambitious). In any event, I sewed the two together to make the cushion cover – a good example of mixing techniques – paint and print – and patterns.

TIPS FOR WORKING WITH POTATOES

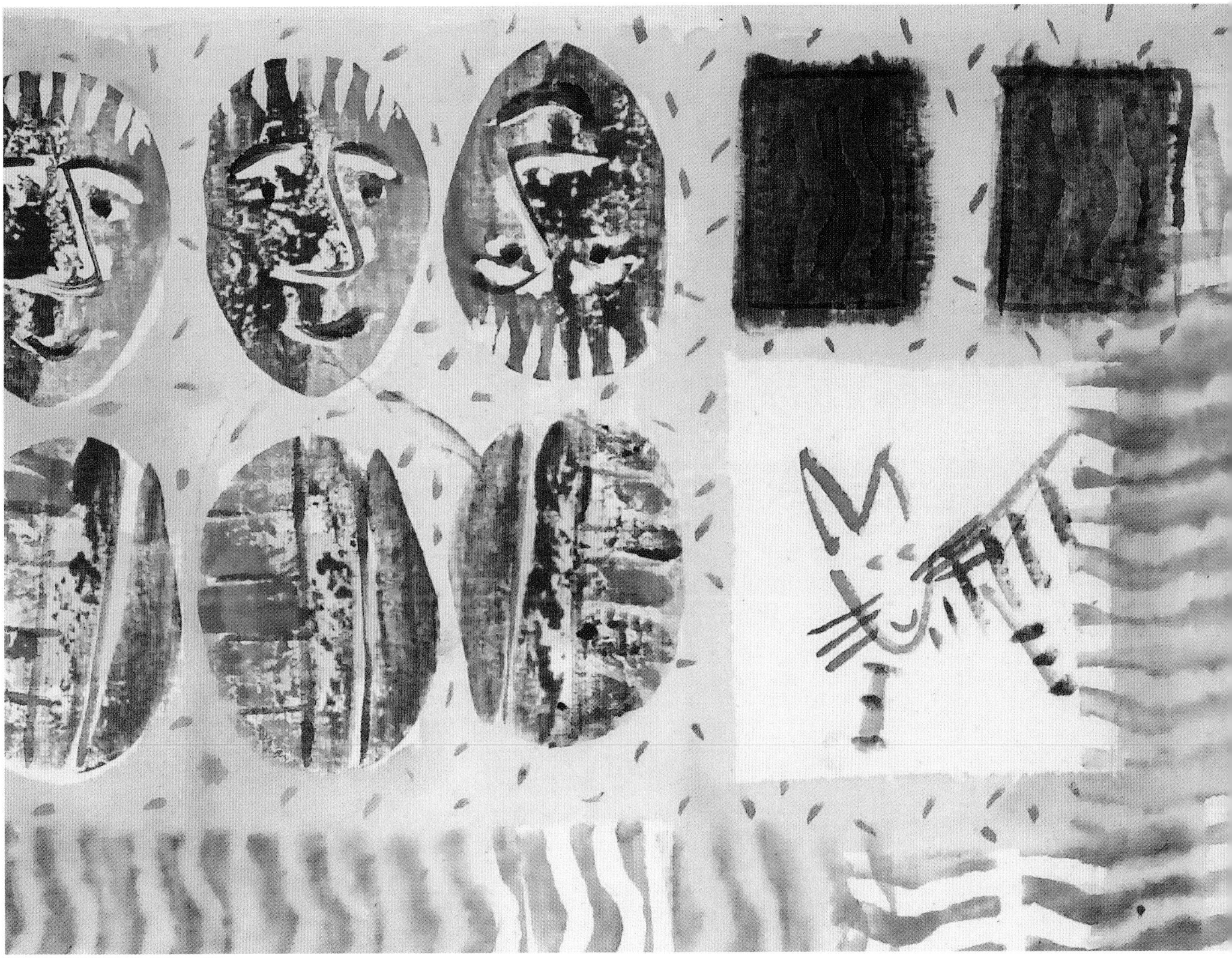

Potatoes will work well for a little while, depending on what you get them to do, but they can degrade quite quickly. If I want to use a cut over two days, I wash and dry the cut potato, wrap in foil and leave in the fridge overnight. If you want to change colours as you go, you can wash the potato and dry it on a rag or kitchen towel.

Whatever shape you want to cut into the potato, you need to make it simple, just the essentials, and use sharp tools. Recently, a child asked me to cut him a digger – quite a challenge, but I just about managed it.

Above A student asked me to carve out a face for him; it was a very floury potato with a grainy surface and it only worked, I think, when I painted in some detail and gave it a colourful context.

Chapter Three
MASKING TAPES

We've touched on using masking tape to isolate and define areas. It can also be a great help in building up borders, making geometric shapes and developing the designs themselves.

Right This T-shirt shows quite wild patterning contained within informal taped areas; the tape has then been lifted and some bands of the unpainted cloth filled in with red. It was painted during a one-day workshop for young people, where two of the students were good at drawing but so very neat that I really wanted them to break out and have a different experience. Thinking that pictures speak louder than words, I made this rather extreme example there and then, both controlled and wild. They loved it, got stuck in and had some real adventures! There was a lot of mess to clear up afterwards, but it was worth it.

Right Here I've used the tape to make different widths and configurations of stripes – in this case, a colourful decorative grid. Containing the paint between the tape allows you to build bands of varying colours and marks. The red half-circles are made by printing a foam dabber down half on, half off the tape.

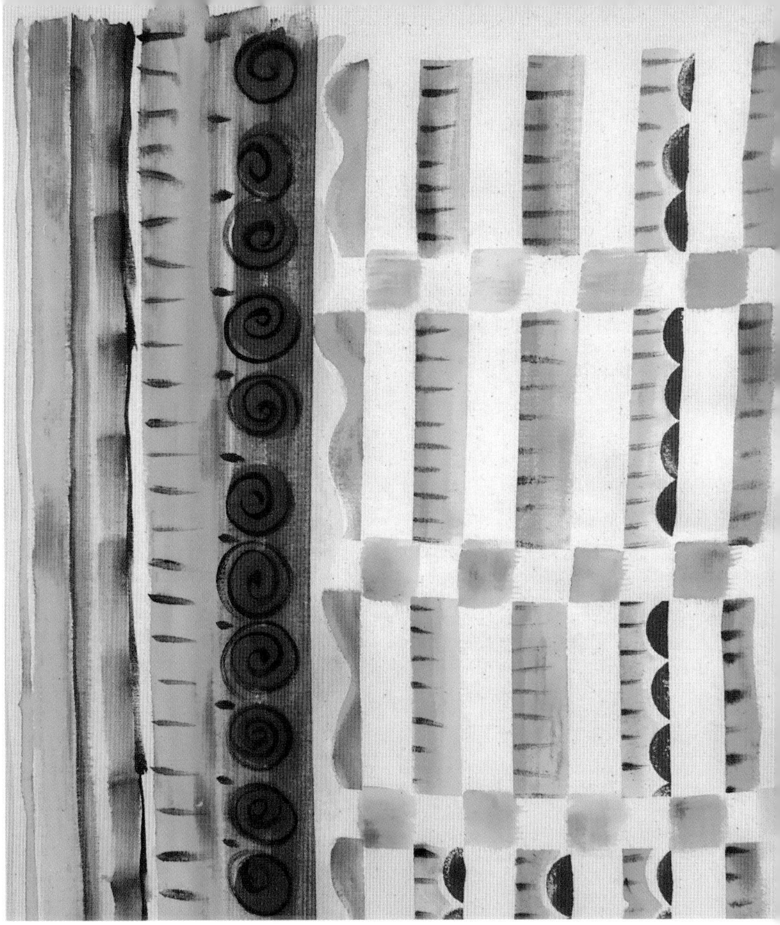

Middle Right To paint the colourful stripes on these T-shirts I put down the tape in a series of parallel strips to give an even distribution across the width of the cloth and to define a straight edge against which I planned to paint. Running my flat brush at right angles to the tape, I used a light stroke as I pulled the colour away onto the cloth, allowing me to build up runs of marks with a clear, sharp edge on one side and a soft, feathery feel on the other. I used quite dry paint for this to avoid the colours running into each other and losing their clarity. When all was done I thought something was missing. I ummed and ahhed and then decided that a fine dark line was needed to give the whole scheme some unity: I painted that on freehand at the end.

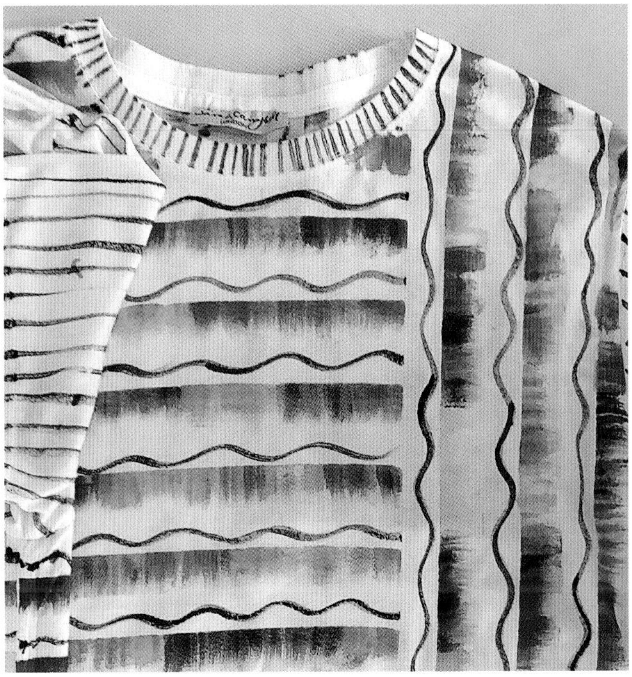

Bottom Using tape on this calico table runner allowed me to juxtapose the sharp unpainted cloth bands 'saved' beneath the tape, with the tonal wash of the colours. The effect is quite intense. The design has an implied table setting in its layout; I remembered I'd designed a series of melamine plates some years earlier and together they make a nice table-scape for an outside lunch (see overleaf).

Project
USING MASKING TAPE ON A SQUARE TABLECLOTH

There are a few things to consider when planning a design such as a table runner or cloth. Do you want it to be the same at both ends or have repeating areas down the cloth? Should it have a seasonal flavour for summertime, Christmas or Easter? Would you like to use a particular colour theme to complement or reflect your room or your plates and dishes?

I'd recently had a sudden yen to unearth some special dishes from the cupboard (I have a small collection of various angular bamboo-themed plates from the 1970s: black, white, moulded and painted). They seemed just the thing to put on my rather arts-and-crafty octagonal two-person oak table, which I think was originally made for a pub garden. I wanted to make a cloth for this table that would sit happily beneath them all. I decided on a square tablecloth with a taped design that would both reflect the angles of my table and plates and complement the black and white colour scheme of my china.

At first, I decided on a very restrained palette of black only for my tablecloth, but I eventually added in some ultramarine and finally a little orange too, to bring the pattern to life.

You Will Need

- Pens or pencils
- Paper
- Cloth, calico, linen or cotton to fit the size of your table
- As large a foam board as can be accommodated
- Pushpins or map pins
- Rolls of masking or low-tack decorator's tape (different widths are available)
- Fabric paints: black, ultramarine and orange
- Brushes: foam and/or traditional
- Sponges: natural and/or man-made
- Hairdryer (optional)

Method

1 Make a small sketch of how you see the finished piece. In this case, I wanted the design to reflect the angularity of both my table and the china, and I happened to have a nice piece of smooth, crisp white cotton that I thought would suit this endeavour.

2 Find the centre of the cloth by folding. For me, it was important to be aware of the centre for two reasons: first, the centre of the cloth would sit on the centre of my table, and I wanted to take account of that in my design; second, the cloth was too big to lay out and paint in one flat piece, so I needed to paint it in sections. Being aware of the centre helped me to keep the pattern under control.

3 Fold the cloth in various squares and diagonals. The creases made will later be used as guides to build up your design with the tape when the tablecloth is opened out.

4 Open out the cloth and pin it onto the foam board, stretching it flat as you go. The vestiges of the creases will remain visible.

5 Tape off the edges with masking or decorator's tape. This will give you a sharp, clear border which can later be decorated or left plain before hemming the piece.

6 Build up your design by masking off areas using lines of tape. Having earlier folded the cloth in squares and diagonals, I used those creases as guides to start to build up my design with the tape when I opened it out. I ran the tape as far as I could diagonally across the design, this way and that, keeping the lines at right angles to each other and remembering that the empty cloth areas would be as important to the design as the coloured lines.

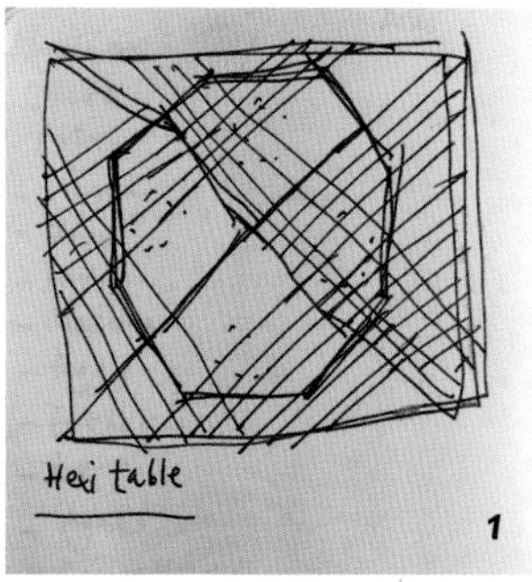

1

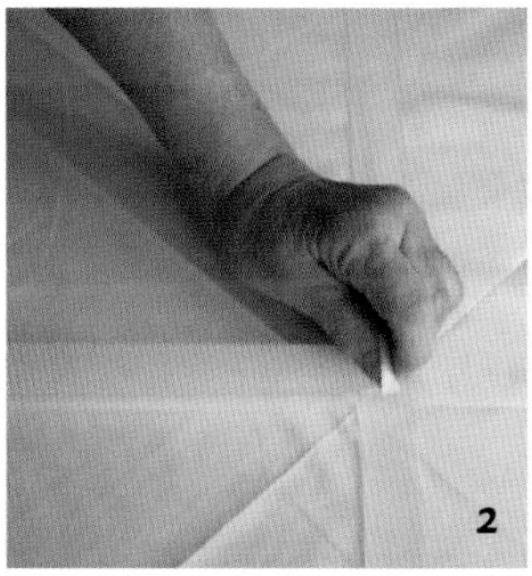

2

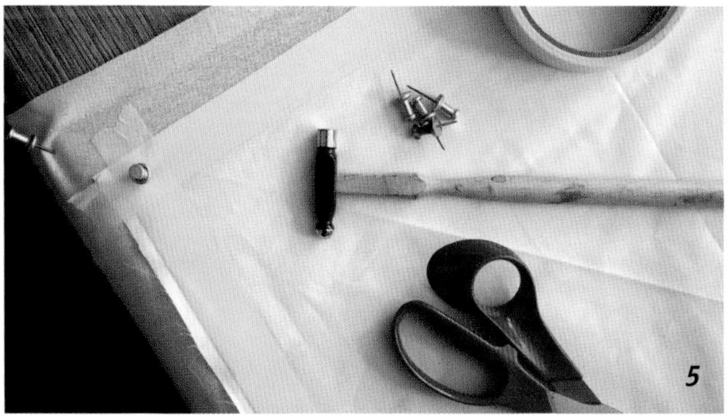

5

7

9

8

10

7 Mix a nice consistency of black paint (not too runny) and paint it between the lines of tape with a flat brush.

8 Be careful to remember where you want to leave the cloth as white space: you can always add in more colour, but it's impossible to remove! I built up the designs slowly, drying the paint with the hairdryer.

9 Partially remove the tape as you go along to see the effect of your design.

10 Having finished with the black paint, leave the design to sit for a while, pinned to the board and propped up. This is always a good ruse – you can quickly tell where the balance of a pattern is out or a particular motif is demanding too much (or not enough) attention. In this case, I quickly saw that the piece needed another colour and I decided to add in some further stripes of bright ultramarine.

11 Tape off some new areas running over and through the black to build up the surface with that lovely rich ultramarine paint. I still needed to be mindful of the white areas – not to fill them up.

11

12 Finally, add in some tiny touches of bright orange. I distributed these highlights evenly across the cloth so that wherever you'd sit at table you would see a bit of everything.

Project
USING TAPE AS A STENCIL

Using tape is also a brilliant way to control and build up stripes, bands and frames, as shown in the Portable Games Board project (see page 50). Sometimes I cut out shapes from within the taped areas, making a sort of self-adhesive stencil. For this neat work, I like to use a decorator's tape such as Tesa, which has a smoother edge than paper masking tape, is easier to cut and will survive painting, lifting and replacing several times. I love the idea that, once it's cut, one piece of tape can go so much further than its given dimensions.

You Will Need

- Rolls of low-tack decorator's or masking tape
- Cutting mat
- Scalpel
- Pens or pencils
- Cloth: calico, linen or cotton
- Fabric paints/inks
- Brushes: bristle or foam
- Hairdryer (optional)

Method

1 Lay strips of tape out on a cutting mat. I used the widest tape I had, 5cm (2in), and stuck the three lengths to the cutting mat. Draw on your chosen design.

2 Cut out your shapes with a sharp scalpel. Simply running a scalpel through the tape and easing the pieces apart gives all sorts of simple design possibilities. I gave each of my strips of tape a different design character, and carefully laid any cut-out pieces on the mat too for use in my scheme.

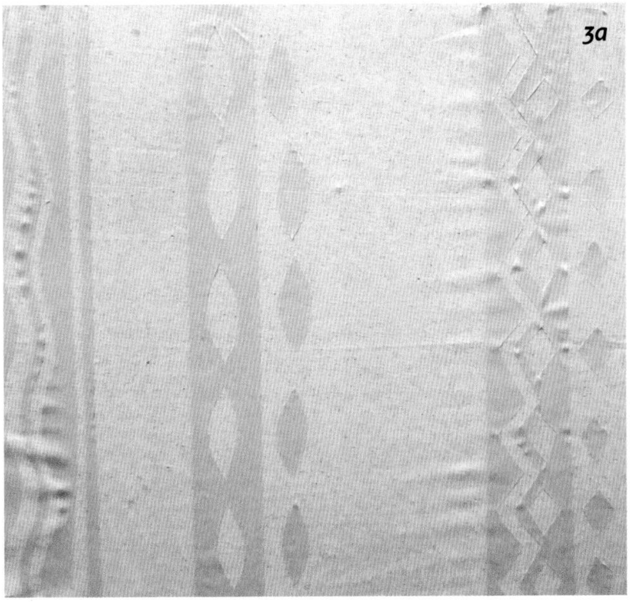

3a

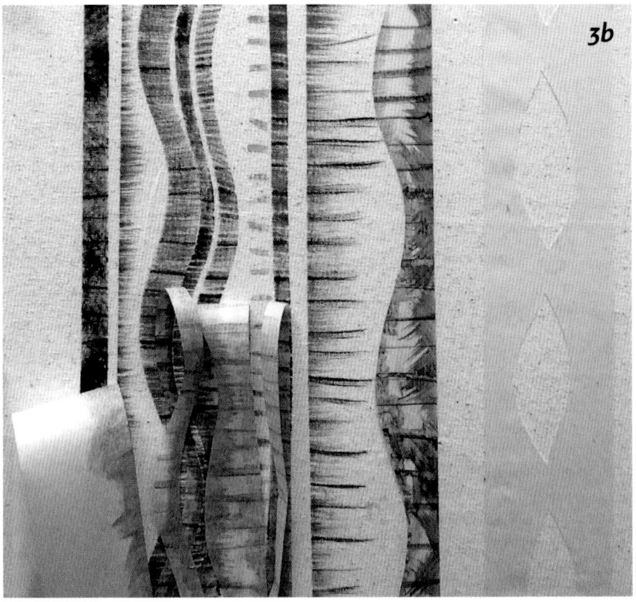

3b

3 The pieces of tape are carefully lifted, placed on the calico and pressed down to ensure good adherence. Now paint your design. I left spaces in between to give me areas to build up the patterns as I go by lifting and replacing the tape.

4 Dry off the painted areas with a hairdryer so you can lift and replace the tape without too much smudging. As the pattern developed, I added in linear elements and overpainting to give the piece some depth and interest.

4

Tip

Remember, that blast of air from the hairdryer can splatter the paint about, so be careful!

USING TAPE IS ALSO A BRILLIANT WAY TO CONTROL AND BUILD UP STRIPES, BANDS AND FRAMES

As with all these projects there is always scope for change, additions and improvements to the cloth.

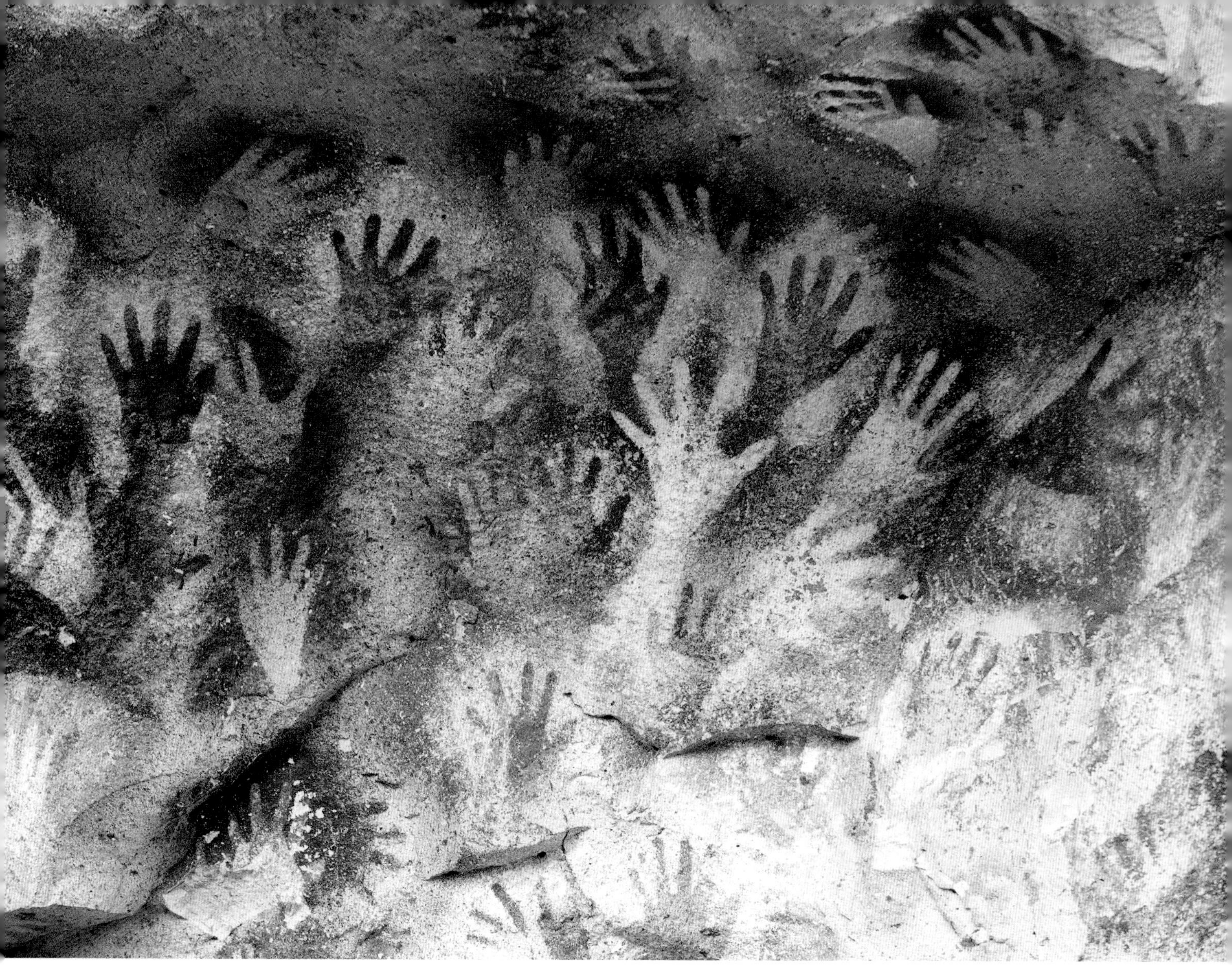

Chapter Four
STENCILS

We humans want to leave our mark: as far back as forty-five thousand years ago, early humans used their hands as stencils on the walls deep inside underground caves, perhaps to say, 'We're here, we're magic.' The extraordinary paintings above were discovered in the Cueva de las Manos in Argentina, and have been dated back to around 9,000 years ago. It's thought the pigment was blown out through a hollow bone.

Stencils have long been used in the reproduction and development of pattern on textile as a template to paint around or push colour and resist through – a system allowing for the repetition of pattern without the need for a printing machine (though, of course, a screen print is fundamentally a stencil method).

Above These are little nineteenth-century Japanese stencils, notched for accurate printing register, with written calligraphy notes and a tiny cut-out corner triangle for easy storage. They show different designs for the *Mon*, or family crest.

Below A venerable *haori* kimono, dyed indigo with the clan emblem resist-printed through one such stencil. The message, though small, is clear for all to see – another case of 'Here am I.'

From this hands-on-hands graffiti to the most refined Japanese *Katazome* and *Katagami* paper stencils used with paste resist to the everyday stencils I cut and use, the principle remains the same. The use and reuse of stencils give consistency of image – a sure-fire way to build a reliable pattern.

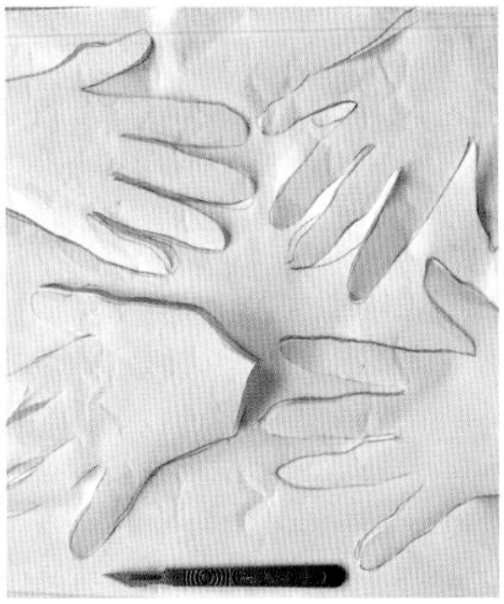

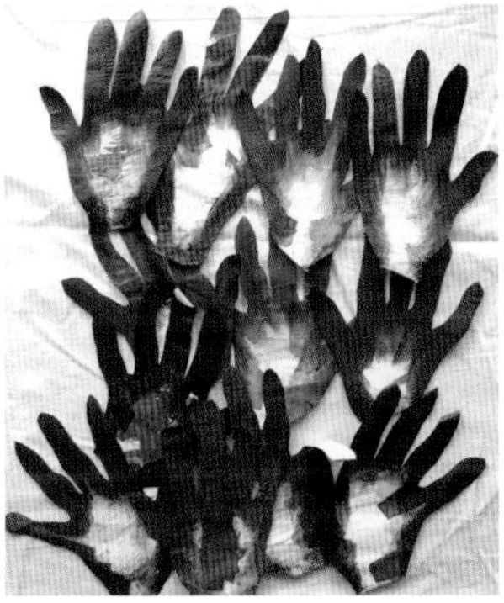

Those ancient hands inspired me to make a piece of my own using freezer paper stencils (see page 82). I drew around my own hands on paper and cut the shapes out to make the templates.

Top I painted around my hand stencils onto a piece of linen, placing and replacing them again and again.

Above Right These were the stencils once I'd finished.

USING STENCILS

The three basic materials I use for my stencils are card, paper and freezer paper. I do occasionally use polyacetate stencils too, especially for paste resist work (I have once had these cut to my own design by a laser-cutting company). I like to use stencils in a variety of ways, as follows.

Right To allow for well-spaced motifs on a painted background.

Far Right To build up a surface patina of pattern.

Bottom To make a continuous consistent design which can change and develop over a large area.

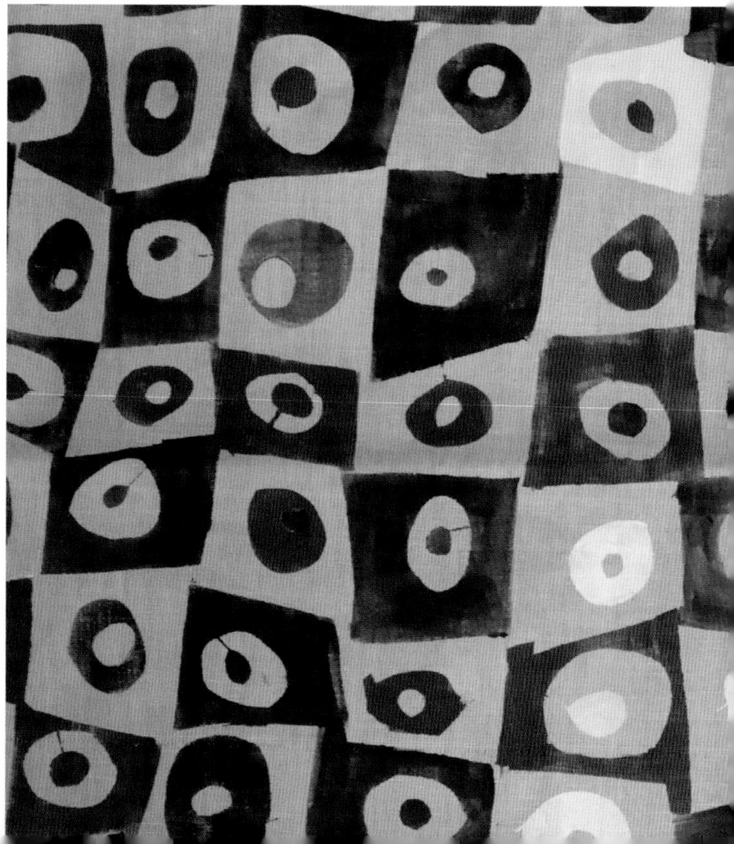

Above Of course, there are plenty of ready-made materials to hand to use as stencils – this little horse was painted round a Mexican tin decoration.

I use my own hand-cut stencils. Although these can be cut from any sort of paper you have available – even newspaper will do for a short-lived or spontaneous project – I use traditional stencil card when I can. This is sturdy brown card treated with linseed oil to give it strength and longevity; but that also makes it quite a challenge to cut!

There are different approaches to the actual cutting out, and this impacts how you may want to use your stencils. To retain both the positive and negative shapes – such as the flowers and the shape they leave behind when you've cut them out – it's best to use card and a sharp scalpel. When I have a long project I collect six or so scalpels together and put new blades in each, then I can work through for quite a while without having to stop to replace them. You really do need a sharp cutting edge to make a good line, and using a little pair of pliers helps to change the blades safely.

Using scissors and paper can give a more fluid cutting motion to make the positive image, but it may be harder to retain the negative one – the space from where you've cut it. This may not matter; it depends on how you want to build your pattern. Tearing the paper stencils gives a different effect again. Cutting with pinking shears or perforating with little holes and splitting like a postage stamp can also be intriguing techniques. The same principles of cutting apply to using freezer paper stencils, though I use the stencils themselves in a different way, as I will show. Here is a straightforward project to start with, using stencils cut from card.

Project
MAKING A COTTON PANEL FOR A FUROSHIKI BAG

This project, a small bag, tied in the Japanese Furoshiki style, requires a simple square of hemmed fabric; in this case, it has been painted using shapes cut from traditional stencil card. Calico is quite a sturdy cloth for this purpose (very often a softer, more pliant fabric is used), but it will do the job. When tied, the pattern makes a visual impression rather than a placed statement. The painted panel could also be used as a scarf, bandana or small tablecloth.

You Will Need

- Piece of oiled traditional stencil card
- Several scalpels fitted with new blades
- Small pliers, if you have them
- Cutting mat
- 1m (39in) square piece of calico (I hemmed it before starting)
- Brightly coloured fabric paints
- Brushes

Tip

Other card can be used, but the advantage of the oiled traditional stencil card is that it can be used many times.

Method

1 Cut the floral shapes from the stencil card on a cutting mat, lifting them away carefully and retaining the spaces they leave. I wanted to build up the pattern using both the positive and negative floral shapes.

2 Having mixed a palette of bright colours, start work in the middle of the cloth (you can see I have marked the centre with a tiny purple auto-fade pen cross), holding the stencils down by hand and painting through and around the cut shapes. I used a dryish brush to apply the colour so there was no splurging.

3 Overlap the stencils as you proceed in order to build up a flowery patina of colour. To keep the colours clean I used a different brush for each one. Between applications it's good to dab the stencil between two sheets of kitchen towel just to remove any excess paint. I worked towards the edge, turning the cloth as I went so that I could reach it easily.

4 When the piece is dry, paint in some little details with a fine brush – dots and dashes give the flowers extra definition and perkiness.

5 Around the hem, paint a border of little black dots to finish off the design. When the cloth is folded into a bag (see opposite), these edges make a nice difference to the knotted corners.

This is an all-over pattern that can be folded in any which way. You could also plan one with borders or stencils in a more purposeful layout to complement the square shape or the shape of the folded bag.

Here's how to fold and tie the cloth into a bag:

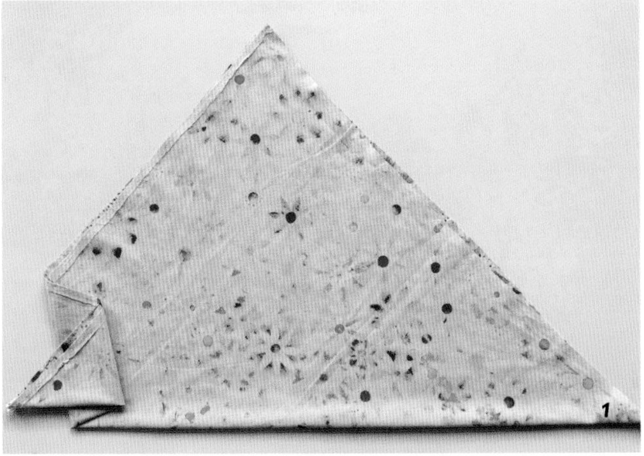

1 Start with the patterned side facing you, then fold the square of cloth in half across the central diagonal to make a triangle so that the 'wrong' side faces up.

2 Make a knot in each of the two corners of the long fold, keeping them equidistant. These will form the sides of your bag.

3 Turn the knotted cloth right side out, and pull it to a long diamond shape with the knotted corners at the middle point.

4 Tuck the knotted ends into the sides, and tie the other two ends together to form the bag's handle.

5 Pull the handle knot taut, shake the fabric down and voilà, there's your bag!

You can find much more information about this online (see page 176 for a suggested video).

STENCILLING A DRESS LENGTH

For this project I used quite a large linseed card stencil cut as a vase of flowers; it's one I've reached for several times for different projects and it has survived a lot of painting. I've cleaned it more than once by wiping it down with water – due to the oiled surface, it has survived! Along with the large stencil, I used a set of floral shapes that have also done good service. I wanted to make a dress length with an overall floral design, but this time place the large motifs very deliberately along one edge to give a border at the hem. I have often designed border prints for commercial printing for both dress fabrics and bedlinen.

None of the detailed colour placement in the vases and flowers on the dress is exactly the same: this gives them a lively uniqueness yet retains visual unity. With hand-painted fabrics, trying to make an accurate repeat runs somewhat counter to both the practical possibilities and the spirit of bespoke that gives the process its charm. Consistency in a pattern does not have to rely on exact mathematics or measuring: replicating the 'feel' of the motif across the piece will do. Practising repetitive mark making, as shown at the start of this book (see page 32), is a great way to get the feel of making a reliable rhythm.

I knew I wanted quite a graphic look and so decided to make the dominant colour black. In this instance, I used a sponge to apply the paint – this is a better method when there are fine lines to negotiate.

Left Having pinned out a length of calico, I began by using the vase stencil, placing it at regular intervals to make the black outlines and shapes along the selvedge. When that was dry I switched to using brushes and painted in the colours; all the vases being some arrangement of blues and with different levels of brightness in the flowers. Having dried the black, I could run the paint over and around the lines, giving a cheerful bold look.

Right Taking the other cut floral stencils, I set about covering the main area of the cloth. Continuing with the graphic black as the dominant theme, I used both the positives and the negatives of these stencils to give variety. When dry, I scattered the bright colours across the field to give emphasis and focus. Just a small dab in the right place can show us a flower.

Left Finally, I painted a bold blue band at the very edge, beneath the softer blue vases, thus giving the pattern some visual weight.

Above I've used this particular vase of flowers stencil several times, including for large panels and other garments on soft linen.

Above I've sometimes also painted in a background colour, as on this large panel. Here you can see a variety of colour thoughts on one piece. I like the red/yellow, yellow/red ideas, but I haven't taken them further – yet.

Chapter Five
FREEZER PAPER STENCILS

Another way to make clear, defined shapes and areas on fabric is by cutting stencils from kitchen freezer paper. This paper is sold on a roll, like aluminium foil, and is available from kitchen or cookware shops and craft stores.

Freezer paper is thin but strong. It can be layered up or folded so that several stencils may be cut at the same time. Shapes are cut and then ironed onto the cloth with a hot dry iron so that they adhere to the surface. Be sure to place the shapes shiny face down – that's the side that sticks. Once the cloth has been painted, the shapes can be easily lifted and repositioned several times and, again, ironed into place. This needs to be done with care, though the pieces are actually surprisingly durable and I've often used mine many times over. They do curl up once painted, but then flatten out again with the iron, and they also eventually lose their stickiness. But they're great while they last.

This method has a very particular look and works where you want to make clear sharp shapes and silhouettes, or to mask off areas in order to retain blank cloth while painting in a coloured ground. Here are some examples using freezer paper:

LINEN JACKET

Left For this fine dress-weight linen (I aim for around 150–250gsm) I cut the freezer paper into long fine strips and ironed them onto the fabric to define the diamond areas. I then painted the coloured bands within them by hand. This gives movement within quite a formal layout. This material has a natural deep linen colour of its own and the bright colours seep in, retaining their vibrance without being jarring.

Right I used the fabric to make a long jacket, which I really enjoy wearing. For this, I painted the pieces to fit to the shape of the paper pattern before it was sewn, so there was no wastage. I also painted the front facings, collar, cuffs and pockets to make a completely bespoke and pattern-specific garment. This really is one of the perks of painting your own clothes.

LETTER FORMS

On this sample you can see some ideas using letters, numbers and sympathetic shapes built up into a random pattern. I've tried several thoughts out on this one piece of linen, from the plainest (bottom right) to overpainting with gold, or with only red and then with many colours. These stencils also give you the opportunity to paint areas of continuous textures in the background.

FLOWERS

I've used these cut-out flower shapes several times in different ways. Each iteration has been adapted and coloured for its end use.

From silhouettes...

...On linen for hand-painted cushions...

...To coloured flowers for a cotton smock...

...And on book cloth for a special handbound album.

Project
USING SIMPLE RED DOTS

Dots, spots and circles are always charming. Using freezer paper stencils on calico, I made quite a large area of a simple spotted pattern which I then painted into with a brush, adding different colours and details. This whole piece is another good example of a cloth whose design reads as consistent but is not measured out mathematically. It would make an interesting skirt or top.

You Will Need

- Freezer paper
- Sharp scissors or scalpel
- Template or circle shape to draw around (optional)
- Iron and ironing board
- Calico fabric for your project
- Board or surface on which to pin your fabric for painting
- Fabric paints
- Brushes: rectangular and fine point

Method

1. Cut lots of disc shapes, retaining the paper from which they were cut as completely as you can. You can cut freehand or draw your shapes on the matt side of the paper – through a template or around a lid, or perhaps use a compass. I cut my circles freehand with scissors, but it depends on what sort of shape you want and how confident you feel.

2. Iron the dots onto the calico, as both positive and negative circles.

3. Paint the whole piece scarlet using a rectangular paintbrush – a foam brush might hold too much water, which could seep beneath the paper stencil and compromise the sharp outline.

4. You may wish to lift and replace the dots several times to extend the pattern.

5. When this part of the painting is dry and the stencils are all carefully lifted and laid aside, go back into the pattern and add other colours and details. Some of mine were drawn with a fine brush; others were more robust.

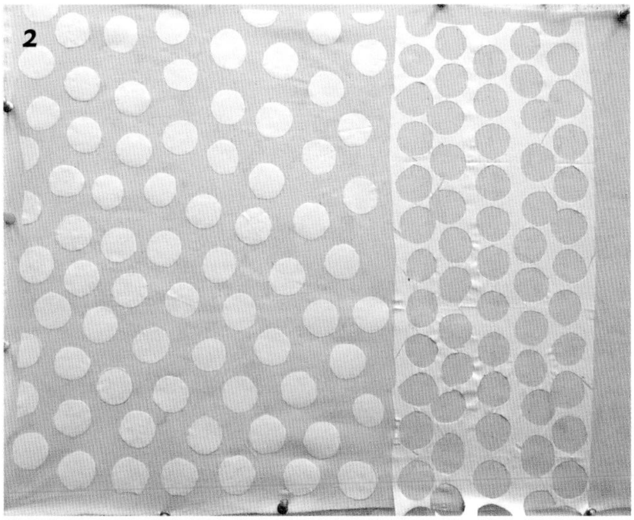

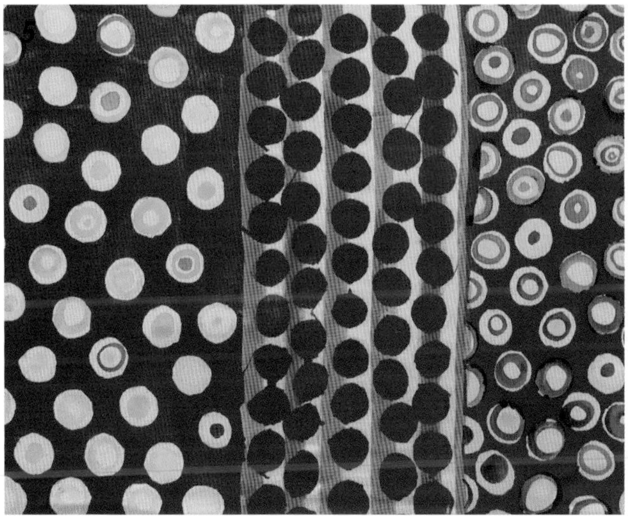

This area became part of a much larger piece using different coloured grounds and showing all sorts of dots and circles using a similar technique. Some of the areas within this large pattern were created by running lines of masking tape down the cloth to make divisions for the different colours; when lifted, I filled the resulting empty bands with dots made with a foam dabber (as seen on page 20). These marks have a slightly different nature to the others and add to the lively feel of the surface.

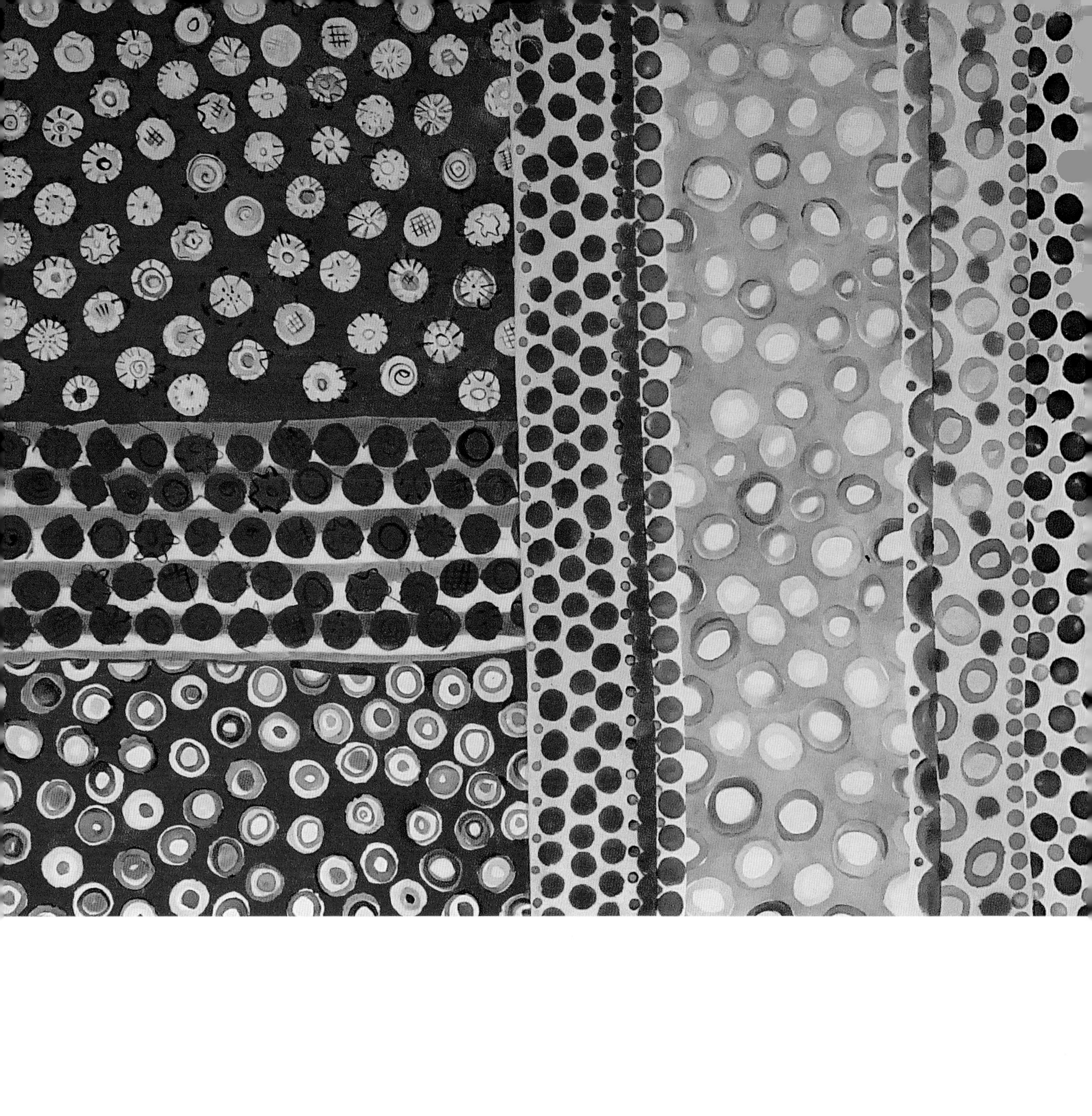

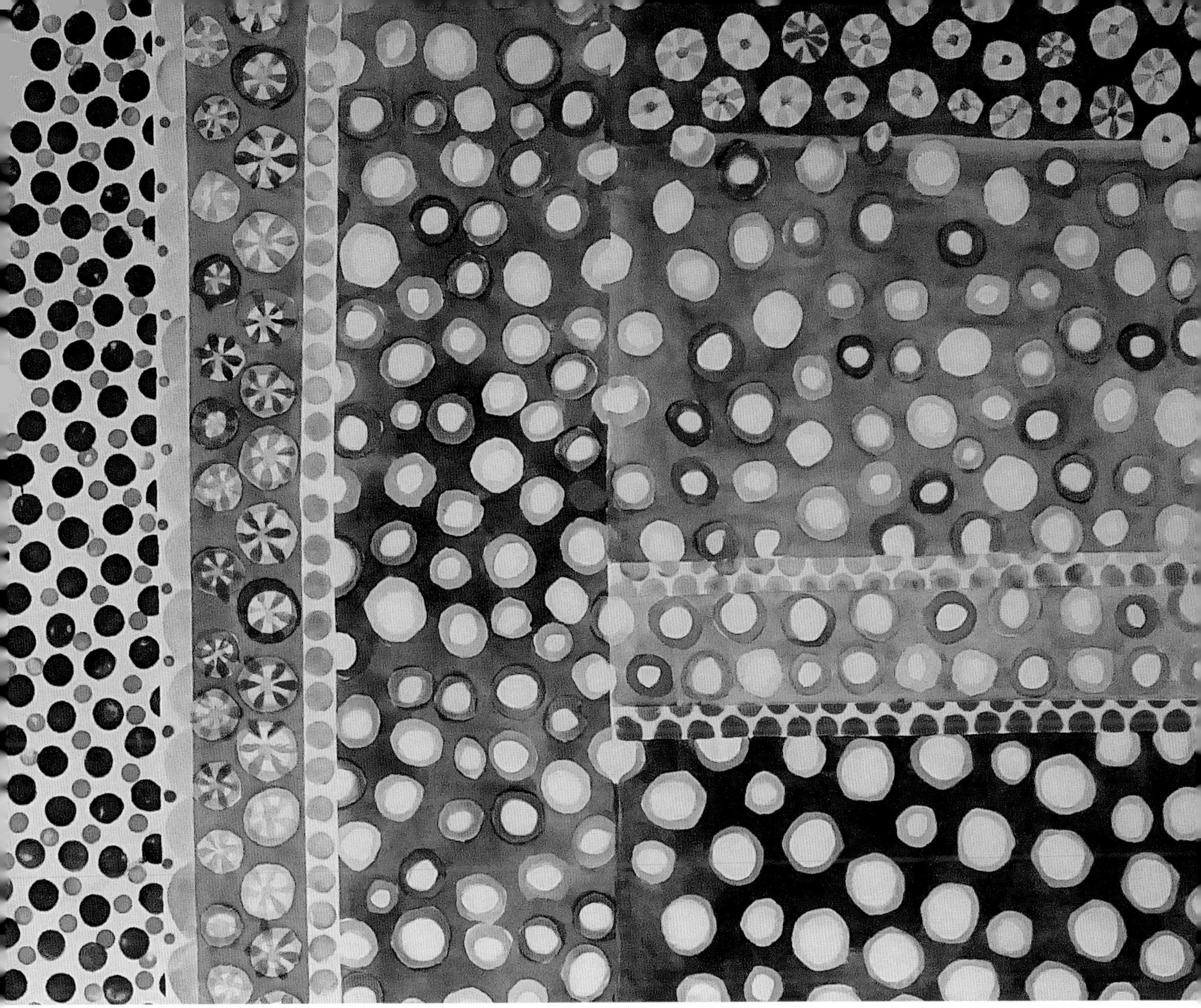

ANOTHER WAY TO MAKE CLEAR, DEFINED SHAPES AND AREAS ON FABRIC IS BY CUTTING STENCILS FROM KITCHEN FREEZER PAPER

RED AND BLACK LEAVES

I'm very fond of this bit of cloth. I wanted to make a piece of fabric that clearly showed the positives and negatives of the shapes I was painting.

Cutting a rectangle of freezer paper folded double, I loosely drew the leaves with a pencil on the matt side of the paper and cut them out with a sharp scalpel on a cutting mat, retaining the sheet so that I could paint through as well as paint around the leaves.

The freezer paper tends to curl up as you work, but don't despair – it flattens out with the iron. Here are my pieces ironed onto a length of calico. In fact, as I had cut two pieces at once, I had enough for the two colours I proposed using. By folding the paper, the shapes make mirror images of themselves.

I began by scattering the leaf shapes on my cloth, spacing them evenly and turning them hither and thither as I'd cut them, to give movement and interest to the design. To apply the paint for this project I used a natural sponge as I wanted some texture. I first sponged the red paint on around the ironed-on leaf shapes to make the background, and then when dry I used a brush to add detail and dimension before peeling off the stencils. The peeling off is very rewarding as the sharp silhouettes are revealed in the very textured ground – a dramatic contrast.

Above Then I painted the other area – where the leaves would become red and the ground would remain as cloth – the stencil for which I had carefully ironed onto the calico. I finished off with painted details; lifting this bigger area of freezer paper needs care in order to avoid tearing the more fragile parts.

Above Right It's exciting to see the pattern emerge from the rather messy stencil.

Right The two charcoal areas came next to complete the piece. Here the tonal ground is painted with a brush, more as a linen texture, with outlines and spots worked into it too.

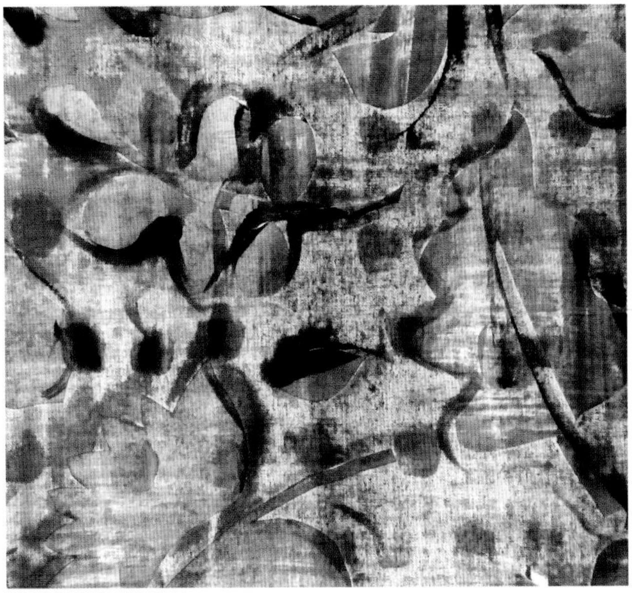

Left You can clearly see the dramatic juxtaposition of 'shapes present' and 'shapes absent' in this design – and it's a good example of how much value one can derive from only a few colours.

TWO STENCILS, FOUR CATS

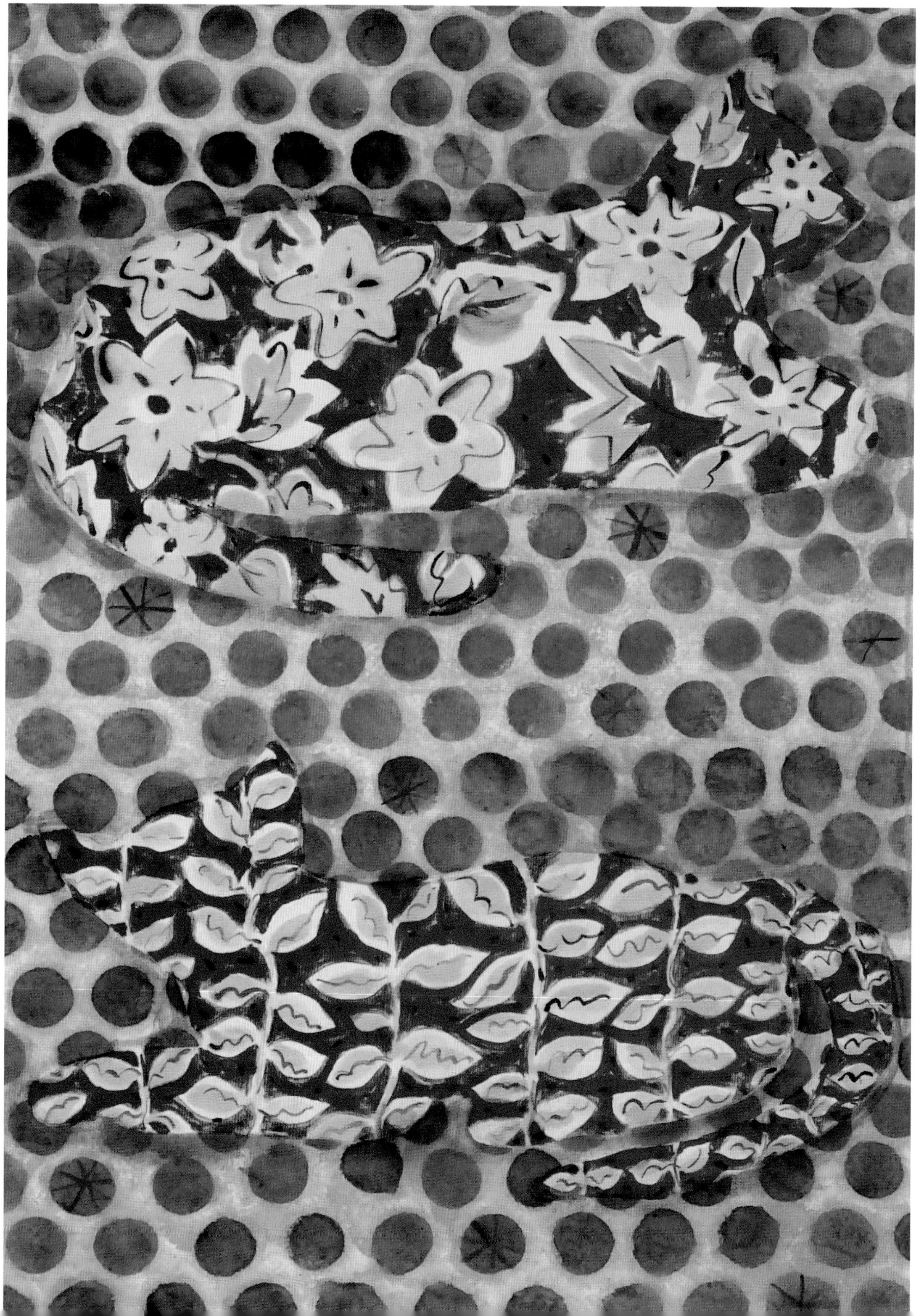

There's always a good time to make some fabric gifts, and knowing that a few feline fans would soon be needing presents, I drew and cut two large cat-shaped silhouettes, facing in opposite directions. As I wanted to paint patterns both within and around the shapes, I also conserved the paper surrounds. They did get a bit scrappy, but I carefully kept all the pieces so I could iron them into place on the cloth when the time came.

Some time earlier I'd bought a few ready-made cotton tea towels so had one to hand, which I stretched and pinned onto a 10mm ($\frac{3}{8}$in) foam board.

I mixed my colours with the idea of making a cool blueish background with contrasting warm colours for the cats. Having ironed the cat shapes onto the tea towel, I applied a light-coloured tonal wash – not too watery – and used a round dabber to build up the circles in the background.

I then removed the silhouette stencil and, when dry, patched in the background freezer paper with the iron so I could confidently paint the patterns onto the cats themselves. I wanted floral and leafy patterns, contrasting their warm red and yellow colours with the cooler blue ground.

I used those same stencils again, this time ironing them onto linen to make two cushions – one cat curling round each cushion. These are envelope cushions – the fabric wraps around and tucks in at the back. This means they can be painted in one long piece; there are no side-seams, and no zips either – just a seam top and bottom and hems on the raw edges! These cushions are for pads that are 50cm (20in) square.

Tip

Remember to iron your stencils on before pinning – the heat is not good for the foam board or the polythene sheet which covers it.

Having made a sketch in my little book, I measured the linen and pinned it flat. This cloth has a strong natural colouring and the paints tend to sink into it slightly, so I wanted the colours to sit in harmony. I mixed a palette of indigo, rust, amber, charcoal and saffron.

The process was much the same as for the tea towel – ironing down the freezer paper silhouette stencils, painting the patterned ground and then lifting, swapping the stencils and painting the cats themselves. As with all my work, what happens on the cloth can dictate how the piece progresses; in this case adding the white towards the end of the project was important in brightening the pattern imagery.

Left The colours look beautiful in the autumn light.

Above Tiger looking grand with his smart stripes!

THERE'S ALWAYS A GOOD TIME TO MAKE SOME FABRIC GIFTS

Chapter Six
STENCILS AND PASTE RESIST

There are many ways to make patterns that use the technique of a resist to control how and where the colour lands on the fabric. A resist does just what it says: it creates a preventative barrier between the colour medium and the cloth. A stencil is one obvious way to do this; a print screen is another. In this section I'm going to look at using a simple paste resist applied directly onto the cloth in a variety of ways, and then coloured with paint – all doable on the kitchen table.

Resists are very commonly used all over the world – they are a traditional way of making patterns on fabric using dye, with paste resist mixtures being made from mud, corn, potato, rice or other starch – and, of course, the noble art of wax resist batiks.

Below A magnificent *Ndop* cloth from West Africa. Stitch resist indigo-dyed hand-spun cotton strip woven cloth, used for demarcating ceremonial space, Bamun people, Cameroon, mid 20th century.

Photo courtesy of Adire African Textiles, London.

EXAMPLES USING PASTE RESIST AND STENCILS

I mix a very simple flour and water paste, which can be applied in a variety of ways; fifty per cent flour and fifty per cent water will do, beaten to a smooth, pancake-type batter consistency. If I'm working over a few days, this will keep in the fridge. A foam board or other surface covered in plastic sheeting or newspaper is a good idea as things can get quite messy. Forks, sticks, spatulas, woodgraining combs are all very useful tools: I use them a lot to make textures on paper.

I've used both calico and linen for these samples; these pieces of cloth are quite small, but just big enough to make interesting and useful trials that could be stitched into a patchwork if so wished – though, in fact, I made a little pillow from one.

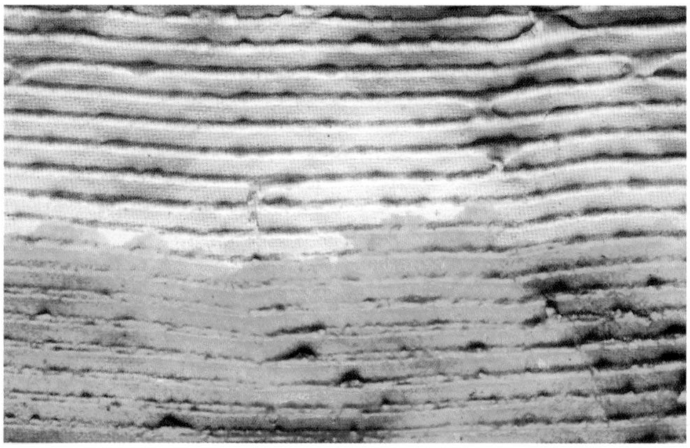

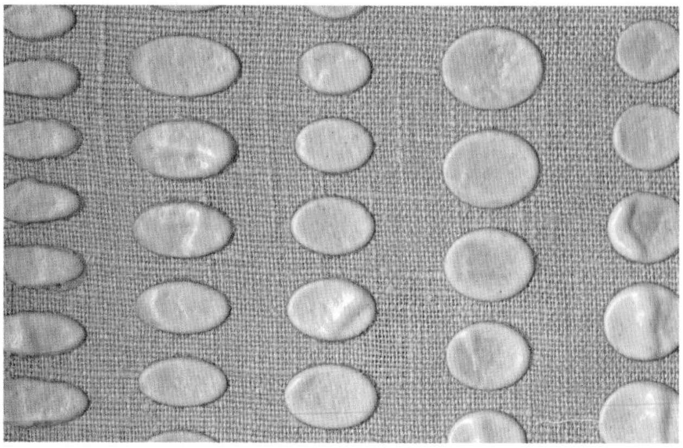

Above For this piece, I used a shop-bought plastic draughting stencil – a template for drawing ovals. Again, I pushed the paste through with the spatula and lifted the stencil – revealing these very satisfactory islands of resist. I dried this on a radiator and then crunched the cloth up a bit, breaking up the paste before painting – this method makes cracks through which the colour can seep.

Above On this piece I've simply spread the paste onto the cloth with a plastic cake-mixing spatula, run the comb through it and then painted colour over when dry. When the paint and cloth are completely dry, the piece becomes quite stiff; time to crack off the resist paste, iron the cloth to set those colours that have penetrated the fabric and then rinse in warm water.

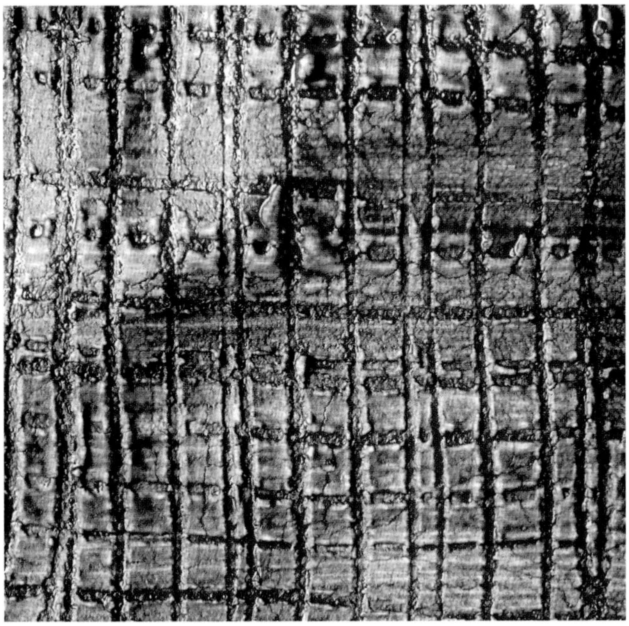

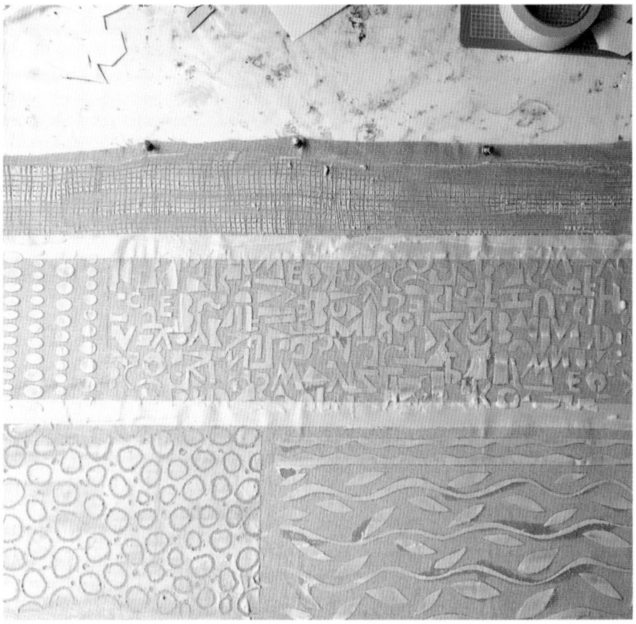

Top Left In this example I combed through a flat application (by spatula) in both directions by dragging a fork through the resist mixture.

Top Right Having had some polyacetate stencils laser-cut for a previous job, I put them to good use with the resist paste. This is one of my experimental linen pieces showing several different parts of the process. Here the paste has been combed or pushed through the different stencils and dried.

Bottom Left Now the painting can begin!

Bottom Right In this last picture, I am standing on the table to photograph the final results, which have been dried, ironed, washed and ironed again!

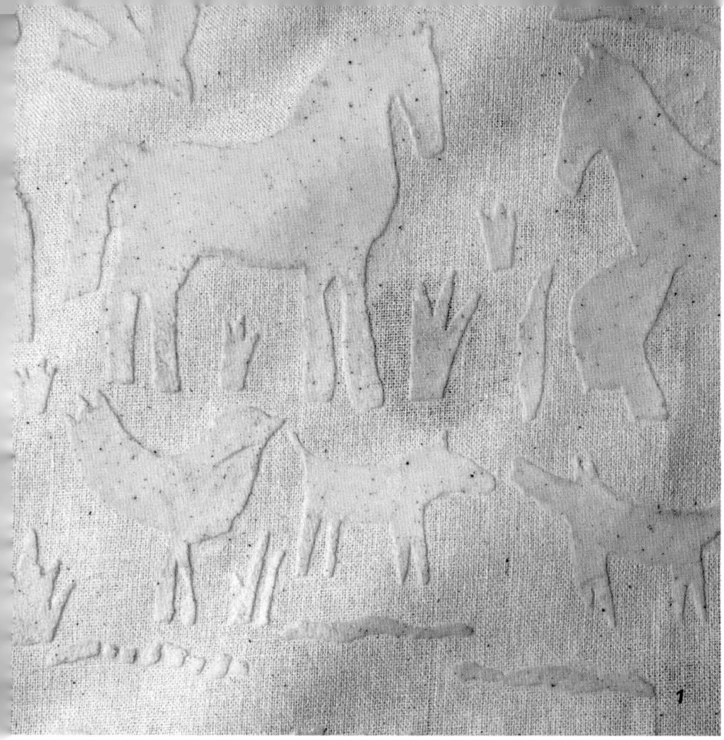

I also used the horses stencil on calico and made a little cushion from the finished cloth.

1 Paste through stencil.
2 The painted surface.
3 Dried, washed, finished and sewn.

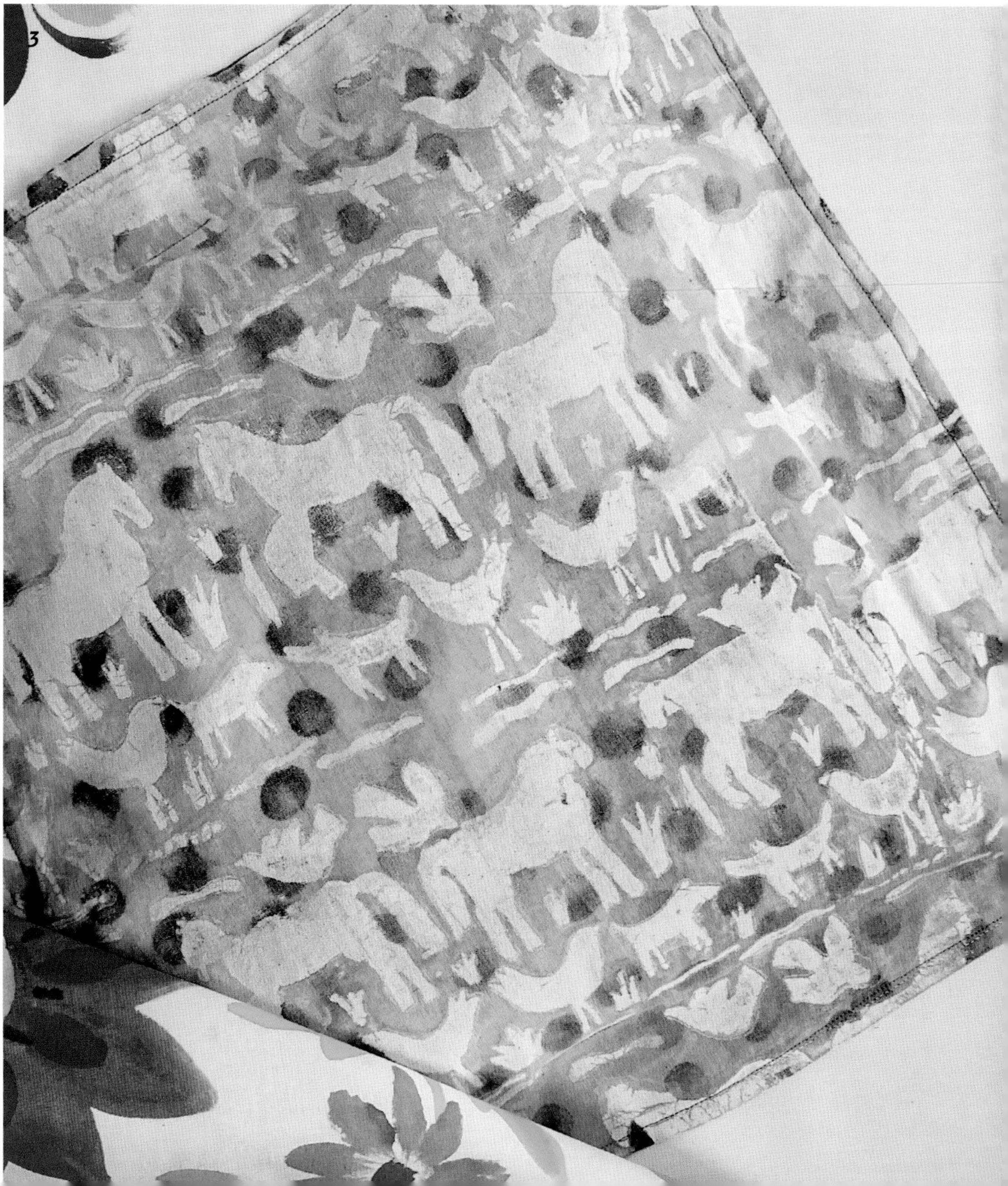

Chapter Seven
SILKS

Painting well on silk is a very skilful and particular pursuit; the fabric takes colour well, but the inks can so easily run into the cloth and go all over the place. Traditionally, silk painters use frames on which to stretch the fabric, pinning the cloth tight like a silken trampoline, and then controlling the areas of ink with a resist such as gutta or hot wax, as used in batik.

Above I do use and teach the frame method – here's an example of a scarf that was stretched and painted on a frame using a gutta resist line – but it's not the subject of this section.

I also paint directly onto silk that has been stretched onto an undercloth or paper surface, not on a frame. This method is a little freer but can have drawbacks if you want a neat, controlled effect.

A very early dress I made gives a good example of how ink can spread on silk if it's not curtailed by a gutta or resist 'fence'. This is a very basic shape – simply two square panels stitched together, with little beads sewn at the neck, and bigger ones (to weigh down the corners) attached at the hem. I stitched this up on the aeroplane on my way to a meeting in New York ages ago, and for a long time it was my best dress – perfect for travel as it folds up to almost nothing!

However, a barrier fluid, such as Jacquard's No Flow, painted on the silk before you begin creates an almost invisible surface or membrane on the fabric that stops the ink from spreading and allows far more control. I used this method for George's fancy silk jacket as seen on page 102.

You can see here the fine lines and neat edges on the areas painted with resist, and how the ink spreads on the plain silk which hasn't been treated.

GEORGE'S SILK JACKET

Here's the story: I received a call out of the blue enquiring whether I painted on silk. Of course, I answered 'yes', and the next thing I knew, an unknown young man came to my door with a very particular request: would I paint the bespoke silk jacket he had in his hand with a jungle scene, suitable for him to wear to a wedding party to be held in L.A. in two weeks' time? I agreed to this, we looked at a few paintings of mine and of Henri Rousseau's, and away he went.

This was quite a challenge – silk being what it is and there being only the one jacket. The first ten days of the fourteen I did nothing about it but think, and then I got to work.

Top Left I realised the only way to feel secure that the inks would behave as I wanted was to use an anti-flow liquid, but I didn't want it to blanket the whole surface. So I painted it under each little section of the design as I went along.

Left I built the whole thing up in layers slowly – it worked.

Above A fortnight after his first phone call, George came by and picked up the jacket on his way to the airport: he was pleased with it, and so was I.

Right I think of this commission fondly – not just because of the outcome but because it required a good deal of trust between us, essentially strangers – on his part that I'd do a good job, and on mine that he'd pay.

Project
PAINTING SILK HANKIES

For little hankies, squares, long chiffon scarves and even ties, I tend to buy ready-made silk items as I'm not great at hand-rolling a hem.

These little pieces are fragile, but they make a sweetly useful and portable painting and are always much appreciated as gifts. The fine filaments of silk yarn encourage the ink to spread fast; I often mix my ink with paint to give it more viscosity, making it easier to control, but I don't like to use too thick a medium on such a delicate fabric.

You could experiment using a gutta resist, but I don't go down that route in this process: it's likely to sink through the silk and adhere to whatever's beneath. Also, as it needs to be dry before you can effectively paint over and around it, the sticking will have occurred before you start painting, causing difficulties when lifting. You could avoid this by putting a layer of plastic beneath the stretched silks, applying and drying the gutta and then removing the plastic and getting to work with the inks. A longish process, but it may be worth a try.

You can also minimise the ink spread by painting the surface of the silk with a stop, like Jacquard's No Flow, or a simple wash of ink, both of which would make a more impermeable surface to hold your painted marks. In all cases, you would need to dry the silk quickly with a hairdryer so that it doesn't attach itself to the pad below. If paper does get attached to the back of the silk, it's curiously difficult to remove.

You Will Need

- An absorbent surface/pad, e.g. calico or wallpaper lining paper
- Silk handkerchiefs (ready-made)
- Map pins
- Selection of foam brushes, paintbrushes and dabbers
- Inks: black and coloured
- Iron

Method

1 To start with, make an absorbent surface or pad on your worktable, either of calico or a soft paper such as wallpaper lining paper. Stretch and pin the fabric onto this surface.

2 When painting little silk hankies or small scarves, you can prepare six or eight at a time. With silk, I use small map pins – these are good as they have no impact on the silk and they don't get in the way of my hand and brush; where there are so many of them, as in this sort of set-up, bigger pushpins would be intrusive.

3 On this set of six silk hankies you could use a variety of tools: foam brushes, paintbrushes and different dabbers. I find it's best not to worry too much about unevenness in the marks; I need to keep the marks light and quick. And I generally work on this sort of group using a limited colour palette. For this group I've chosen to use a black ink as my main colour, into and over which I can paint other colours when dry.

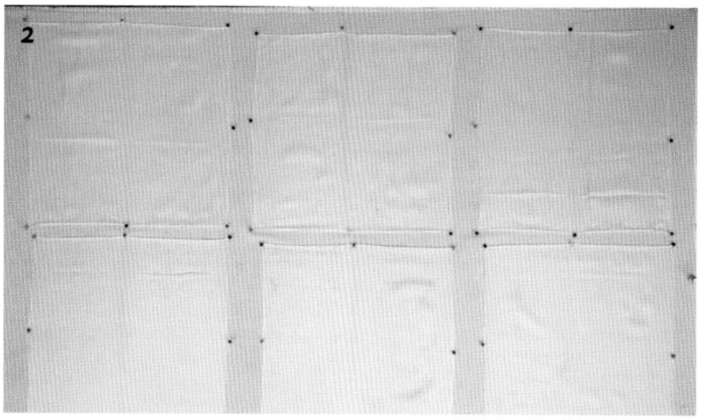

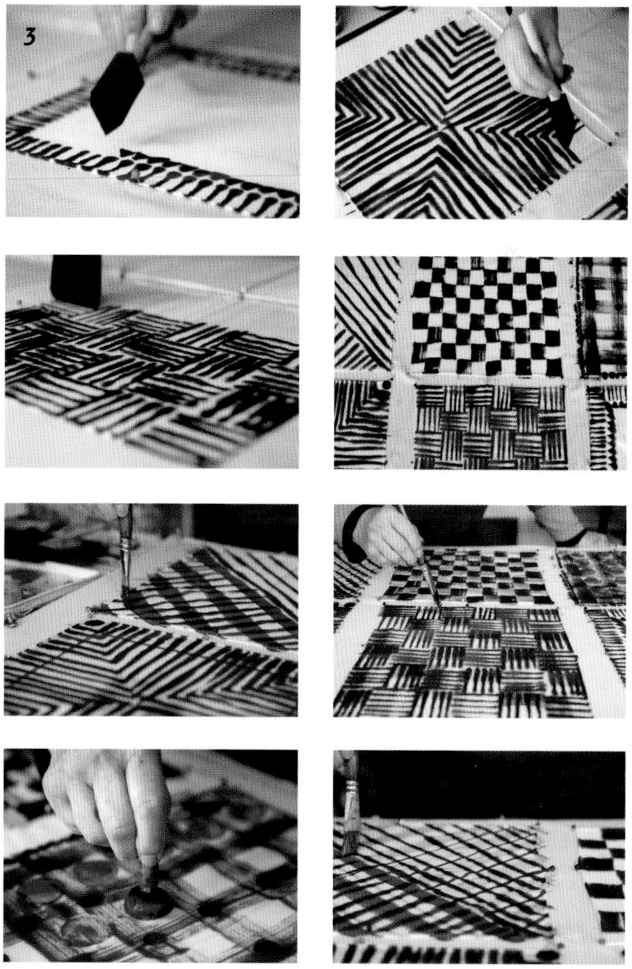

Tip

I tend to keep one implement for each colour so that I'm not having to wash them as I work.

4 Lift the painted hankies quickly so they don't pick up or stick to any of the pad material and leave them to dry before setting the colours by ironing on the reverse.

5 When ironed thoroughly, wash the hankies through gently in warm, slightly soapy water to remove any surplus ink, and then iron again while the silk is still damp.

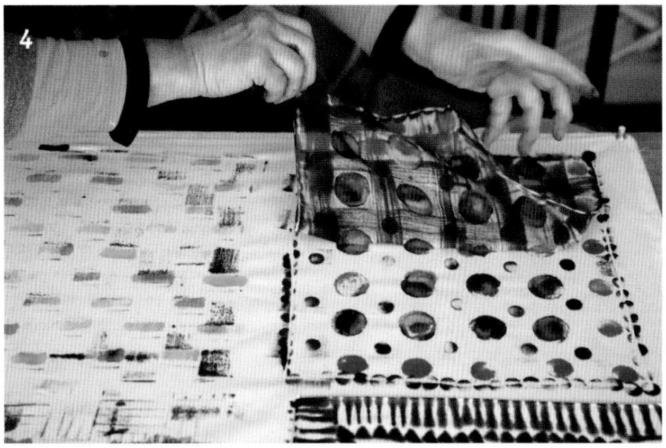

Above The backing paper itself, left with the coloured footprints, can become a lovely work in its own right – you can make it into home-made birthday cards maybe, or wrapping paper. If you've used calico as a backing sheet or pad, you can use the fabric for facings or linings in other projects on the 'waste not, want not' principle. These zipped bags are made from scraps of backing fabrics.

THESE LITTLE PIECES ARE FRAGILE, BUT THEY MAKE A SWEETLY USEFUL AND PORTABLE PAINTING

SILK CHIFFON AND GEORGETTE SCARVES

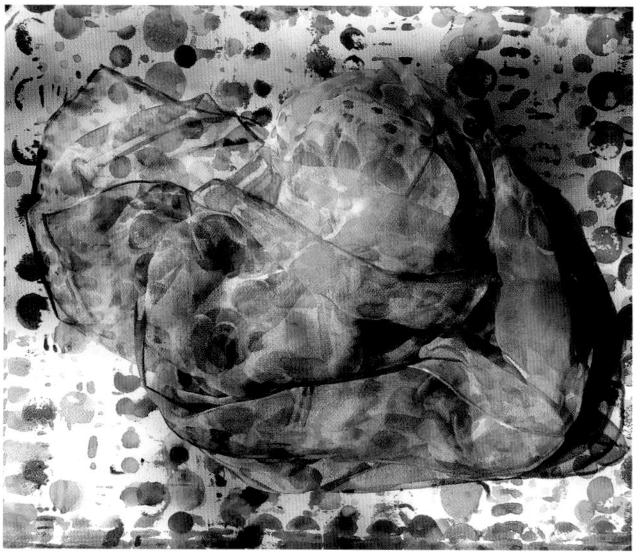

When I paint long chiffon or georgette scarves, I fold them in half before pinning them – the fabric is so fine and sheer that the ink goes through and seems to disappear, but at the end you find you've painted both halves more or less the same! I use foam or bristle brushes, making quite loose consistent marks, and I like to paint the hemmed edge to give some definition.

This photo looks fuzzy – that's because it's showing the two layers of the fabric painted together.

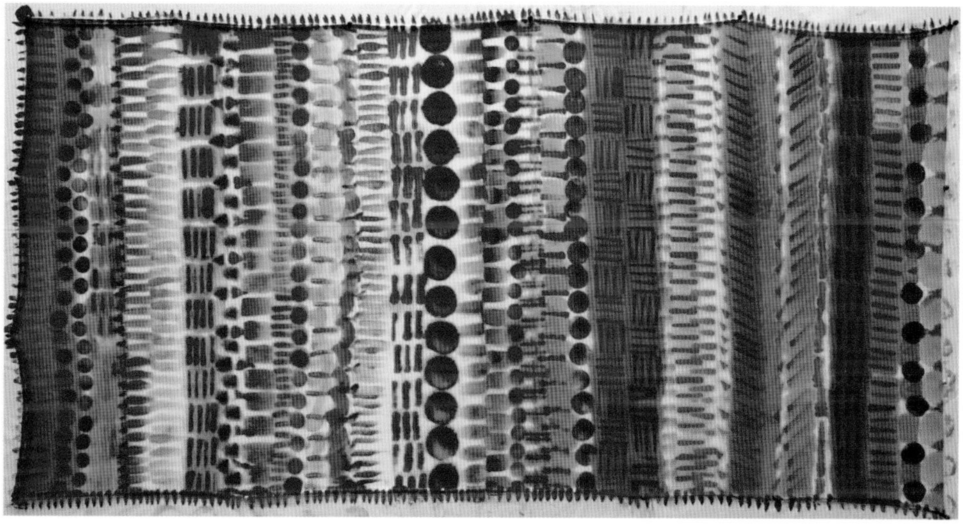

When opened out with the inks set, washed and ironed, it makes a beautiful gossamer of colours.

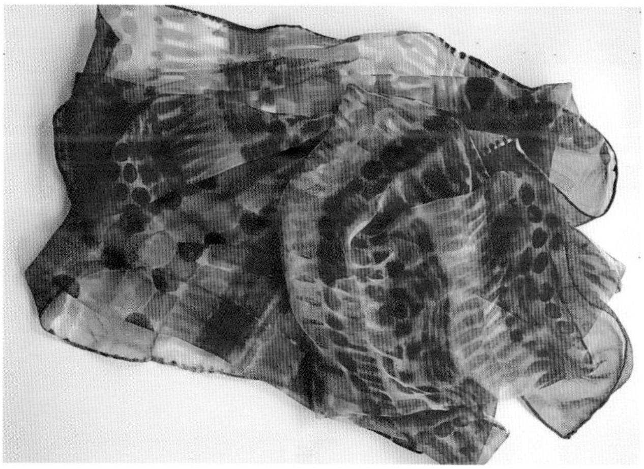

Chapter Eight

PATTERN AND COLOUR PLACEMENT

I often wonder what sells a pattern – is it the colour or the design? Of course, it's a bit of both. It's hard to see one without the other, and the existence of colourways – different colour solutions to the same design – points to the very strong importance of colour and our personal reactions to it. How often does one hear someone say, 'That colour just doesn't suit me' or 'I could never wear red'? These little painted sketches are of the same, very simple design in several colour options; they show what a difference the colour scheme can make. One of the very best things about painting your own clothes and cloths is the control you have on where and how you place the pattern and colour – the decision is yours.

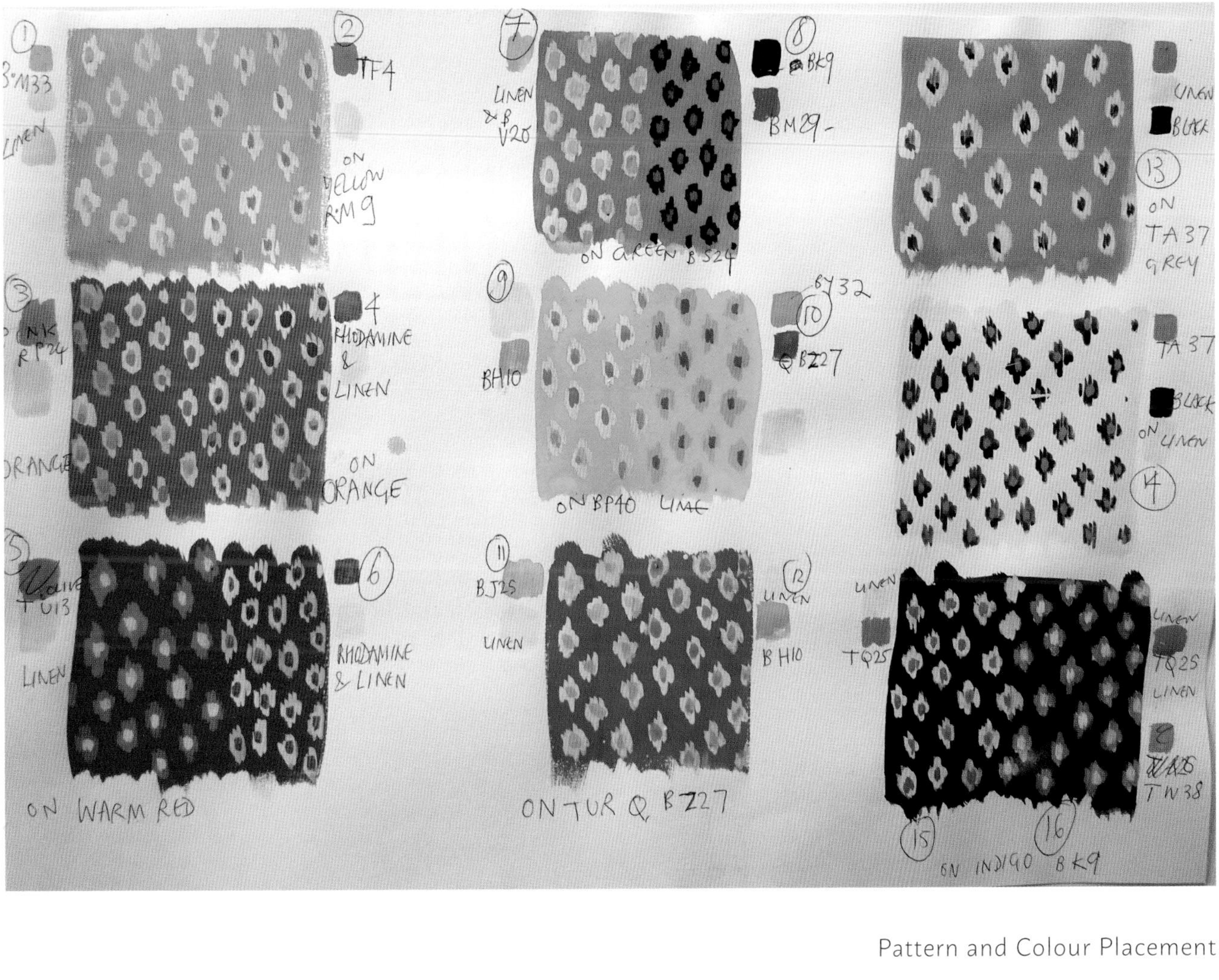

Above These linen lengths show two simple approaches to colour and pattern: one built around the square, the other the triangle. The shapes remain pretty constant, the colour operates in a narrow spectrum (let's call it azure): the interest and effect is in the variations. Being able to make this much variety in the paint colour and depth is one of the great advantages of hand-painting.

I realise I've always drawn, painted and doodled people in patterned costumes and fantasy outfits – I painted this person in about 1965; the line drawing is more recent.

There are at least two major things to consider when planning to paint a garment: the placement of the pattern and the distribution of colour. Of course, these depend on the shape and style you have in mind.

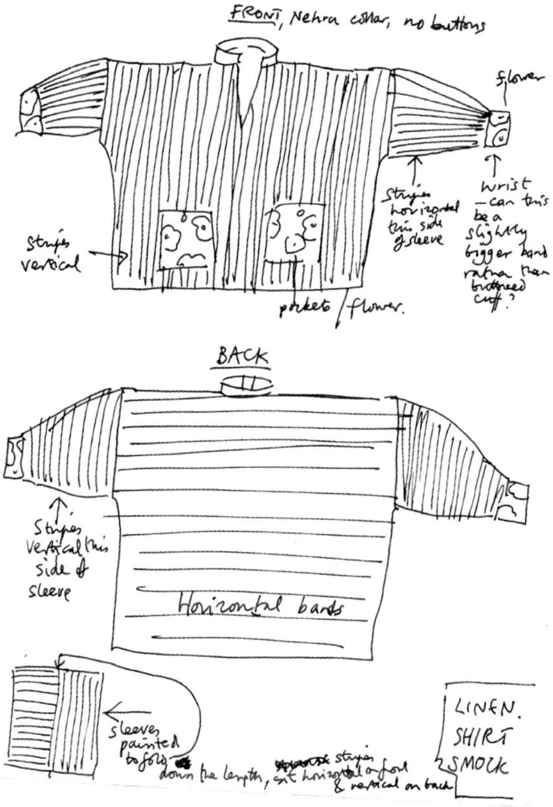

This linen smock shirt works on the simple plan that the hand-painted stripes on the front run down the piece, north to south, and those on the back run across, west to east. The pockets and cuffs use the same colours as the stripes but in a floral pattern. I like these changes, juxtapositions and details.

A LINEN KIMONO-STYLE JACKET

Many traditional and modern Japanese kimonos make full and imaginative use of pattern and colour placement to tell a story, give us a beautiful composition and emphasise the nature of the cloth. This is not a book about sewing; in these next sections we'll look at a very simple garment layout – a riff on the kimono – and how to approach its painting and making.

Our garment is made from a series of rectangles; the measurements and layout are shown on my diagram; the sewing instructions follow later.

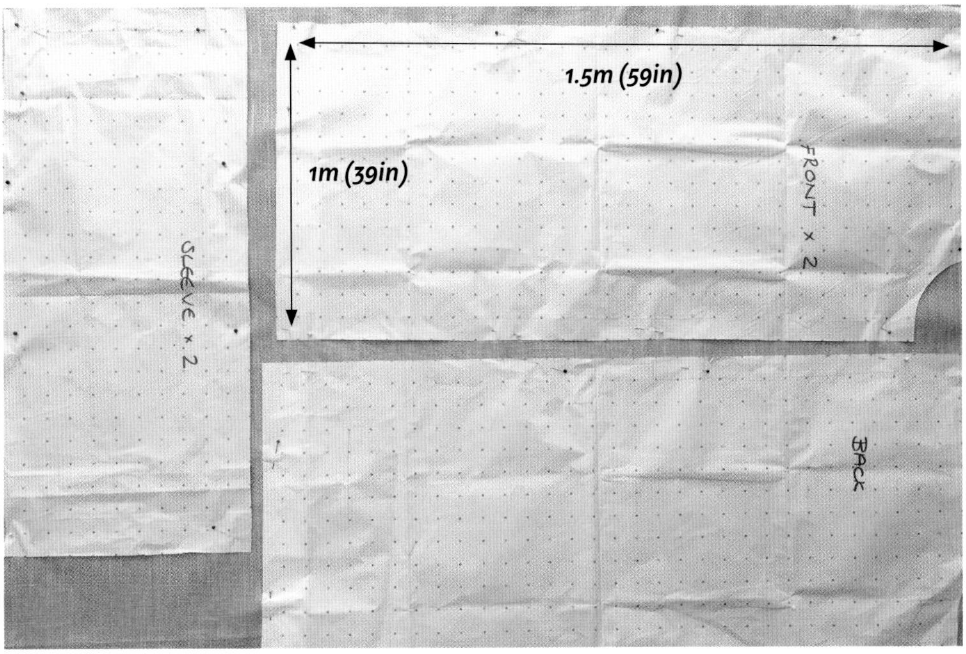

I asked my dressmaker friend, Chris, to kindly devise a simple garment reliant on rectangles (plus a square for the pocket) and she supplied this paper pattern. The fabric, in this case a grey linen, 1m (39in) wide by 1.5m (59in) long, is folded in half longways, as shown.

I wanted to use a dramatic, asymmetric design but with a restrained colour palette to explore how effectively the garment could develop from that simple starting point.

I kept the colour palette limited and consistent, though the paint is applied tonally. I cut the garment pieces before I painted as I needed to make sure they'd match up as planned in the preliminary sketches. This small sketch shows how I saw the painted pattern being placed overall, with the elements – circles and flower heads moving across the garment from front to back in an off-centre layout. I think of these little line drawings as maps to indicate where my brushes might travel.

I'd planned for the design to not only fall asymmetrically, but to distribute the limited colour palette to maximum effect – as the background for the dots and in the foreground for the motifs of flowers and leaves. It explores the idea of positive and negative pattern: the leaf shapes are positives sitting on the fabric, whereas the circles are negatives, seemingly cut out of the painted ground to let the cloth show through. The pocket is an opportunity for further pattern play – in this case a leaf motif, which sits on the spots. That way, I was making the best and most versatile use of a simple premise.

To execute the painting I cut and used freezer paper stencils, as described previously (see page 82). That gave me the excitement of a large and varied pattern and the discipline of the sharp controlled shapes. The question of shape, colour distribution, method and purpose is what concerns me when I start a work of this sort.

Here you can see how the painted panels relate to each other – the front matches, as do the sleeves. The edges are bound, not turned, so the pattern easily reads across.

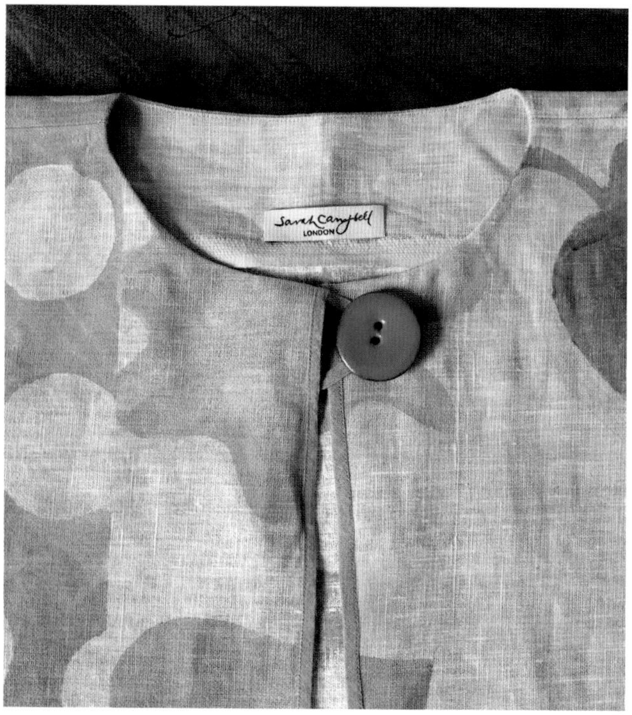

When the panels were painted and the colours cured, I found a button and some bias binding from my French market stash and asked Chris to sew it all up for me.

Process
SEWING UP THE KIMONO JACKET

Here are the basic instructions for sewing up this kimono jacket and the slightly longer version shown in the next chapter (see page 117).

1 If you have a zig-zag stitch on your machine, zig zag all the edges to be seamed. Join the fronts and back at shoulder, 1cm (3/8in) seam allowance. Press open.

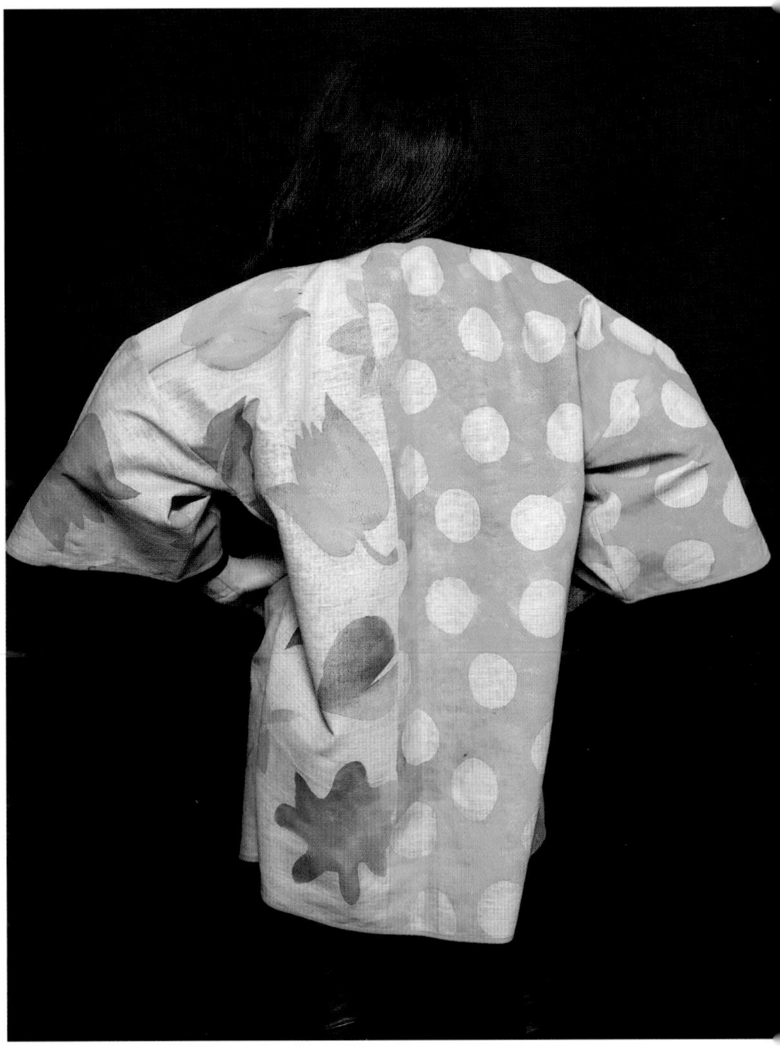

> **Tip**
> If you don't have a zig-zag stitch, bind the seams with bias.

2 Sew the sleeves on and press the seam allowance down the sleeve.

3 Sew from sleeve end to underarm, turn and continue down the body to the hem. Press the seams open. Snip under the arms.

4 Edge with contrasting bias binding. Sew on pocket to finish.

MANY TRADITIONAL AND MODERN JAPANESE KIMONOS MAKE FULL AND IMAGINATIVE USE OF PATTERN AND COLOUR PLACEMENT

Chapter Nine

A PATTERN TO MATCH A PATTERN

COTTON KIMONO

Using the same kimono shape as in the last section, this time I developed a pattern directly referring to the geometric cut of the garment rather than a pattern running across it. A cotton with a smooth crisp surface seemed right for this, cut slightly longer than the previous garment. I chose to emphasise the square cut with differing pattern areas, which were dictated primarily by the rectangles of the sleeves and their relationship to the body of the garment. Although these areas are strictly rectangular, the patterns within are painted freely to prevent any harshness. I also used areas of plain colour which, though not flat, gave relief to the patterns.

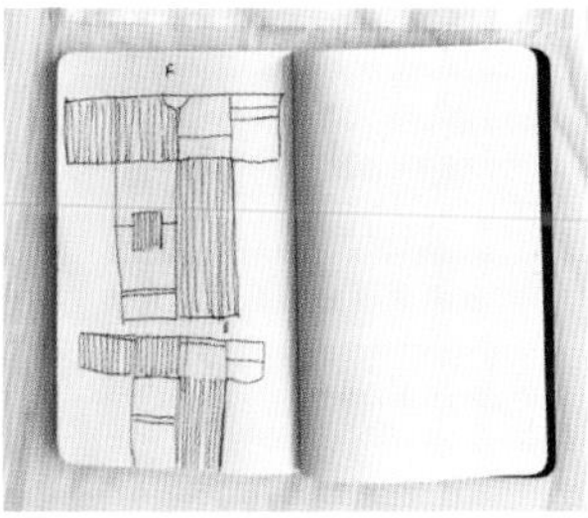

This small line drawing shows first intentions and the logic of the layout, as well as the proposed surface patterning of this cloth. In the end, the design of differing squares became more pronounced.

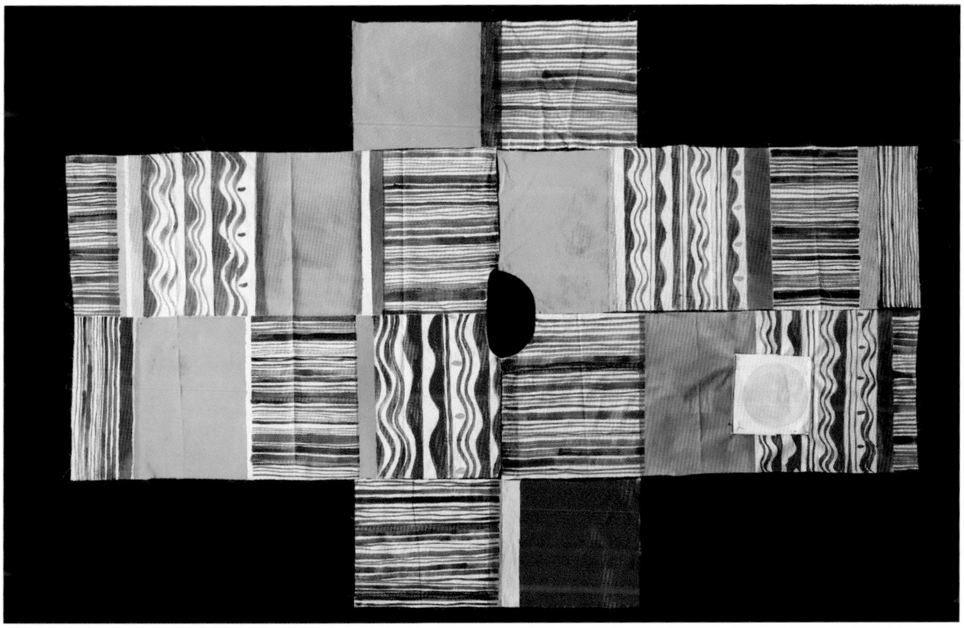

The flatlay photograph of the pieces assembled before stitching shows this chequerboard effect with the plain and patterned squares balancing and counterbalancing each other. I didn't measure the areas, just took my steer from the size of the sleeves.

The paints I used on the cotton bled a little, but I welcomed the softness they brought. As you see here, I also used tape (see page 60) to keep some of the edges neat and straight.

Tip

When trying to keep a fabric crisp and clean it's good to dry the paint as you go along, being careful not to let the hairdryer spatter any wetness across your work.

Fundamentally, the pattern worked as a large check, with fields of plain bright colours alternating with stripes and waves, and narrow colourful bands making the divisions lively.

Project
MAKING A SIMILAR FABRIC

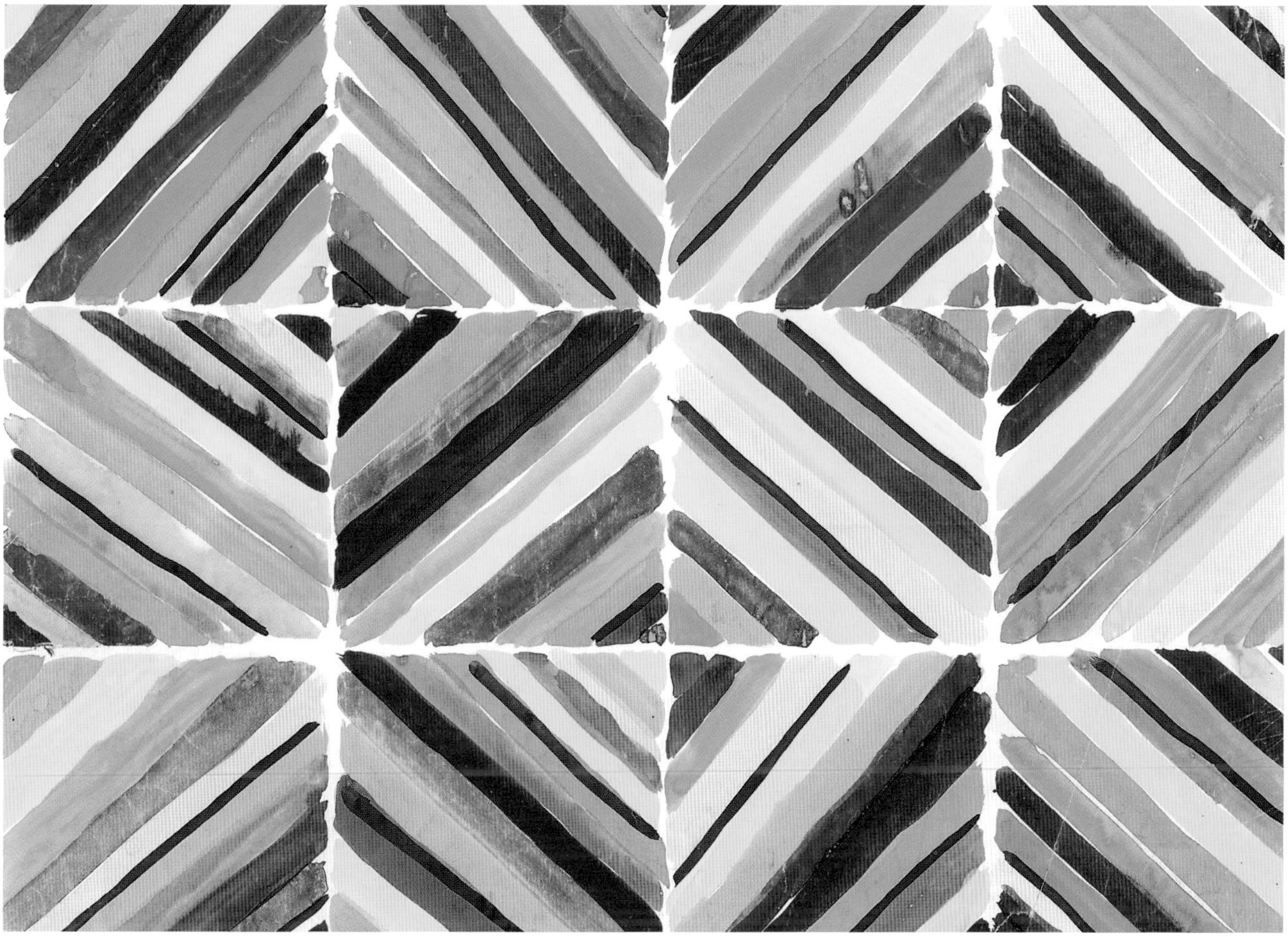

Thinking along geometric lines, so to speak, you could make a similar fabric using the device of folding to give the design structure. This design above, painted within folded areas, is a distant echo of a pattern I painted in the 1970s for Liberty. It was called 'Quickstep' and to make it I started by folding my paper into even rectangles. Those sharp little physical folds served both as a guide for my free paintbrush strokes and a natural barrier to them wandering outside the squares. That pattern had a long and fruitful life in many iterations.

You Will Need

- Piece of cloth (my cotton measured 60 x 130cm/24 x 51in)
- Iron
- Fabric ink or paint
- Palette
- Paintbrush and/or foam brush
- Hairdryer (optional)
- Pushpins or map pins
- Newspaper or kitchen towel
- Foam board

Method

1 Take a piece of cloth – I recommend a smooth cotton. The piece I used was an offcut from the kimono and measured 60 x 130cm (24 x 51in) but a larger piece would be needed to make a full jacket.

2 Fold it carefully into a neat shape – I chose triangular in this instance – and iron.

3 Place the folded cloth on a piece of newspaper and 'paint' clean water into the folded edges to wet them, then seep colour into the dampness. This can be ink or paint, and either a paintbrush or foam brush is effective.

4 When the colour has gone as far as you or it wants, and keeping it folded, dry the piece with the hairdryer or on a radiator and then iron it again.

5 Open the cloth and pin it out flat, retaining the vestiges of the fold creases – these will then be the 'containing' areas for the further patterns and colours of your design as you draw and paint with the water and colour. You may want to refold the cloth and repeat the first process again if your lines aren't clear enough.

6 Taking the lead from the painted squares kimono jacket, I've made a loose geometric of stripes and colour. You could, of course, use this method of pattern division using the folds and without the watery bit!

7 Add additional colours if desired. This whole piece could be just as effective using just one family of colours – the black/indigo look for instance – but I worked across the cloth adding stripes and bands of water and some different colours, more like the kimono jacket.

Above The effect of the original inky folds gives the section divisions an interesting appearance of shadow; and when gathered, the watery lines make pleasing ripples dipping in and out of the surface. Perfect fabric for a cover-up at the beach.

Chapter Ten

PAINTING WITH BLEACH

A trawl through the second-hand shops when I was young would often result in us finding dresses and scarves where the printed patterns – usually flowers – showed as bright colours on a dark background. To get this effect, the cloth is first dyed with the strong colour and then, from the areas to be printed, the dye is discharged (or removed) by chemicals. The motif is then added to those colourless parts of the cloth – hence the name 'discharge print'. This technique is still used commercially, but the chemicals employed have become a little less toxic.

USING BLEACH

A kitchen table version of this process is to paint with ordinary household bleach. As long as the windows are open and I remember to stand back frequently, I really enjoy using it on both paper and fabric – it gives a very particular look.

I use the bleach neat, but you can dilute it with cold or – more effectively – warm water. I have tried an eco-bleach but to no effect, and there are other natural products on the market that I haven't used.

None of the samples below have deteriorated at all over their five or six years, and for all of them I used the household bleach neat. The shirt sustained its corroding damage at the time it was painted and hasn't changed since; it's the only one of these particular pieces to have been laundered regularly.

Some cloths and dyes do not respond at all to bleach, particularly if the colour has been pigment printed, so you need to experiment a bit. Use an inside seam or pocket for this. Man-made fabrics can be stubborn, and some chemical dyes too, but a student came to me with some very exclusive and beautiful deep-dyed indigo-coloured bedlinen from which she wanted to discharge the ground, and, try as we might, we couldn't shift it! I recently bought some second-hand jeans – one pair remained resolutely blue.

When you've completed the bleaching part of the process, rinse the fabric in cold water. You can then neutralise any further bleach action by using a commercial stop, such as Anti-Chlor or Bleach-Stop (bisulfite or meta-bisulfate), or a solution of hydrogen peroxide diluted 1 part to 10 parts water. After neutralising, wash the fabric in warm soapy water and rinse thoroughly. Don't use a vinegar rinse as this can react badly with chlorine bleach.

Tip

It's advisable to wash and dry the bleached cloth before you apply colour, as the fabric paint will need to be heat-fixed with the iron before you can wash the final piece.

Right One very early bleaching adventure happened to this perfectly innocent shop-bought blue linen shirt. I needed to attend a party where the dress code was 'checked shirts'; I didn't have such a thing, so I set about painting one. The bleach worked pretty well, but as it left a pinkish tinge to the fabric I painted some more checks with thick white fabric paint too. I was rather heavy handed – it was late at night – and some of the bleach has since eaten holes in the linen, but at least I looked the part on the day!

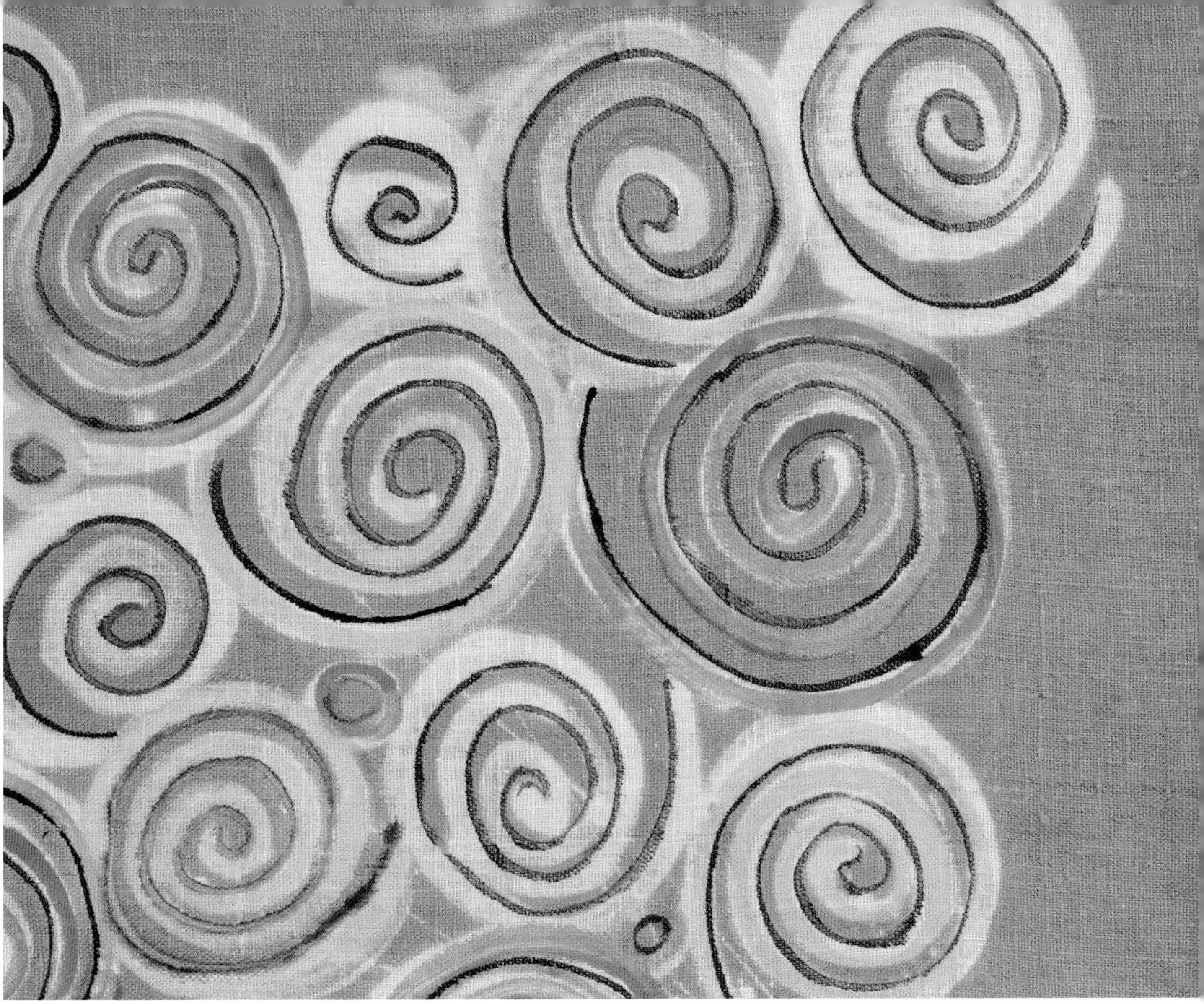

Far Left This experimental piece has a lot going on: a deep navy linen with bleached-out spirals, overpainting and then overbleaching – quite a mess, but very informative.

Top Left These leafy sprigs are some small trials painting bleach onto dyed linen grounds and then painting colour back in.

Bottom Left I painted these samples for a customer at the start of a new collection – ideas to do with paisley and a folk-art feeling. The motifs were bleached out of a black cotton sheeting and then the bright colours were painted back in with fabric paint – not unlike those vintage frocks.

Above Spirals again, this time bleached out of natural-coloured linen, and repainted with orange and yellow, and with a dark defining outline.

Right Here is a little printed pattern from the start of my career to illustrate the 'look'; the flowers discharged out of fine wool.

Project
DECORATING JEANS WITH BLEACH

This little blue dress started life as a cotton petticoat, which I bought from a vintage rail in a French *brocante* when teaching at Chateau Dumas a few years ago. We had a day's diversion spent dying with natural woad (which generally gives a softer effect than indigo) and into the tub it went, emerging this rather sweet blue. This particular cloth and dye are very susceptible to bleach and I had fun painting some huge swishy linear flowers, watching them blossom as I went.

When painting with bleach, set out your workspace as usual, but be sure to open a window or door to get fresh air. It's also good to work on a plastic-covered surface. You don't need to pin jeans: they are quite heavy and you may want to move them around quite frequently as you paint.

Find a jam jar (or similar) for which you have a lid; pour in some bleach and keep it covered until you're ready to work, and also when you have a break or leave your work area. I'm rather particular about securing lids these days – I've knocked over and spilled too many things in my general haste and enthusiasm! A jar or two of clean warm water is also essential – you may want to dilute the bleach if the cloth is very responsive, and you'll certainly need to wash your brushes well. Choose quite a stiff brush that you won't mind damaging – such a thing can happen.

You Will Need

- Pair of old jeans, maybe from a charity shop trawl
- Bleach in a lidded jar
- Jar or two of water
- Lining paper or newspaper
- Dust sheet or big binbag to cover your work surface
- Stiff paintbrush

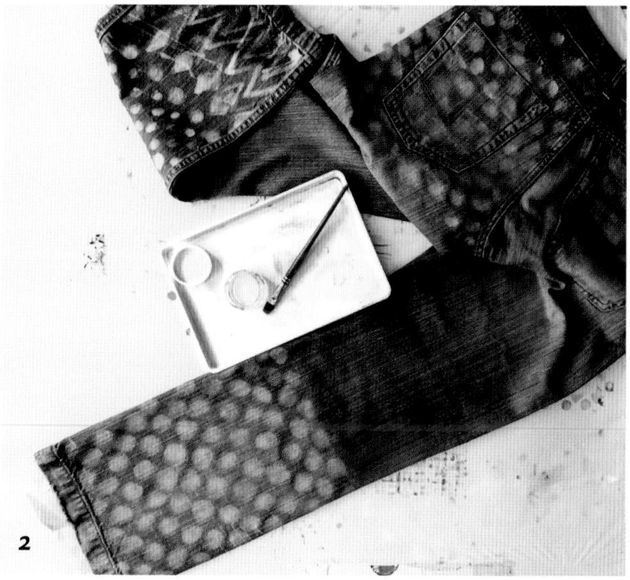

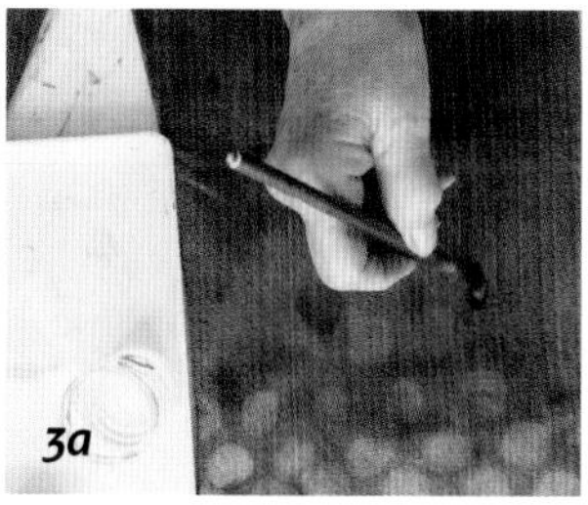

Method

1 Find an unobtrusive part of your pair of jeans – inside the hem, for instance – and paint on a little bleach to see if and how it will interact with the cloth and its dye.

2 Plan your design, line the garment with paper and get to work painting your chosen pattern using a stiff brush. On these jeans I chose to paint spots and chevrons, which were differently distributed on the front and back.

3 You have to exert some pressure to get the liquid into the denim, but then, excitingly, you see the pattern developing as you go along.

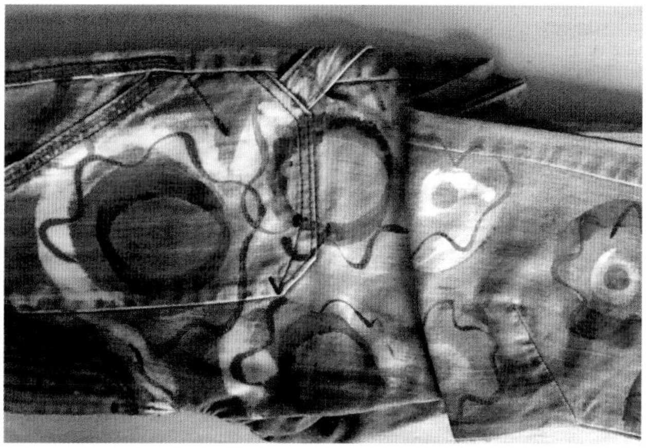

Top Here are the jeans in situ. Juana loved them so much she wore them home.

Bottom For this pair, I brushed the bleach on in rings, big and small, and then painted in additional blue and red patterns. Again, the design varies as it progresses down the trouser legs.

2018 exhibition at the Fashion and Textile Museum.

Chapter Eleven
PAINTING A T-SHIRT

T-shirts have a special place in fashion, as the 2018 exhibition at the Fashion and Textile Museum showed us. T-shirts are garments whose messages can be made overt with slogans, colours and logos; garments with which we can show our true colours, allegiances, history, feelings, even hopes; perhaps garments of true democracy?

Above A T-shirt is an excellent platform for artistic expression too. Here are some I've painted marking occasions, as experiments and as special commissions.

Right Over the years I've taught workshops for both adults and young people – it's great to see students go home wearing their paintings! I love their bold pieces.

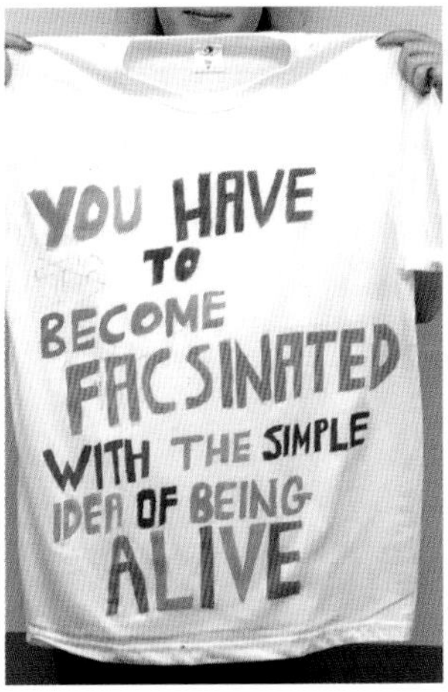

HOW TO PAINT A T-SHIRT

I buy ready-made pure cotton white T-shirts for painting. Before painting any garment you'll need some paper – newsprint, lining or layout paper will do – to place inside the item so the paint doesn't seep through and mark the other side. The paper is also useful as it keeps the shirt in good shape while you work, and while it dries off.

So, for a T-shirt, trace around the garment with a pencil on the paper, cut it to size and slip it inside, making sure it fits snug to the shoulders, sleeves and seams. Dressing a paper T-shirt with a fabric one is quite a funny thing to do, and if you're working with a child on this they can decorate the paper version later, even if it is a bit smudgy – part of a self-portrait perhaps?

I usually paint each of my three grandsons a T-shirt on their birthdays – surprisingly it's 'cool' to wear one of Granny's designs! Over the years we've built up quite a collection – football is always of importance, especially for the two younger boys.

Sarah Campbell
LONDON

THE STORY OF ONE T-SHIRT AND ITS PRODUCTION

My youngest grandson (who was nine or ten at the time) had a project about Indian textiles on the go at school, and for his contribution he wanted to make something to wear: a colourful T-shirt was required.

He had seen a lot of tie-and-dye and printed fabrics and wanted to do something along those lines. So we thought about several methods of 'production' and settled for a tie-and-paint background overprinted with potato prints cut using Indian motifs – paisleys and stars. These are both simple and basic processes and, used with imagination, are bound to be successful.

Top Left For the ties we used rubber bands: he scooped up handfuls of cloth while I twirled the bands around.

control where the colours went. We decided to paint the different colours in bands down the garment – at least on the front.

Bottom Left He brushed the colours on using fabric paints. We had no dye and this was a far easier way to

Bottom Right The back was a little more freeform! We did back, front and sleeves, and we certainly got quite 'painty'!

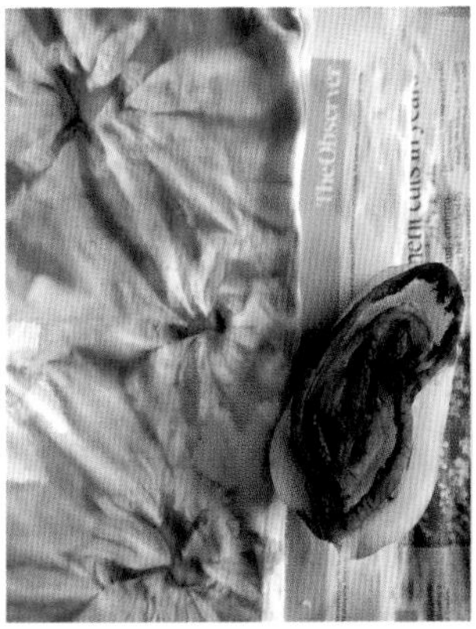

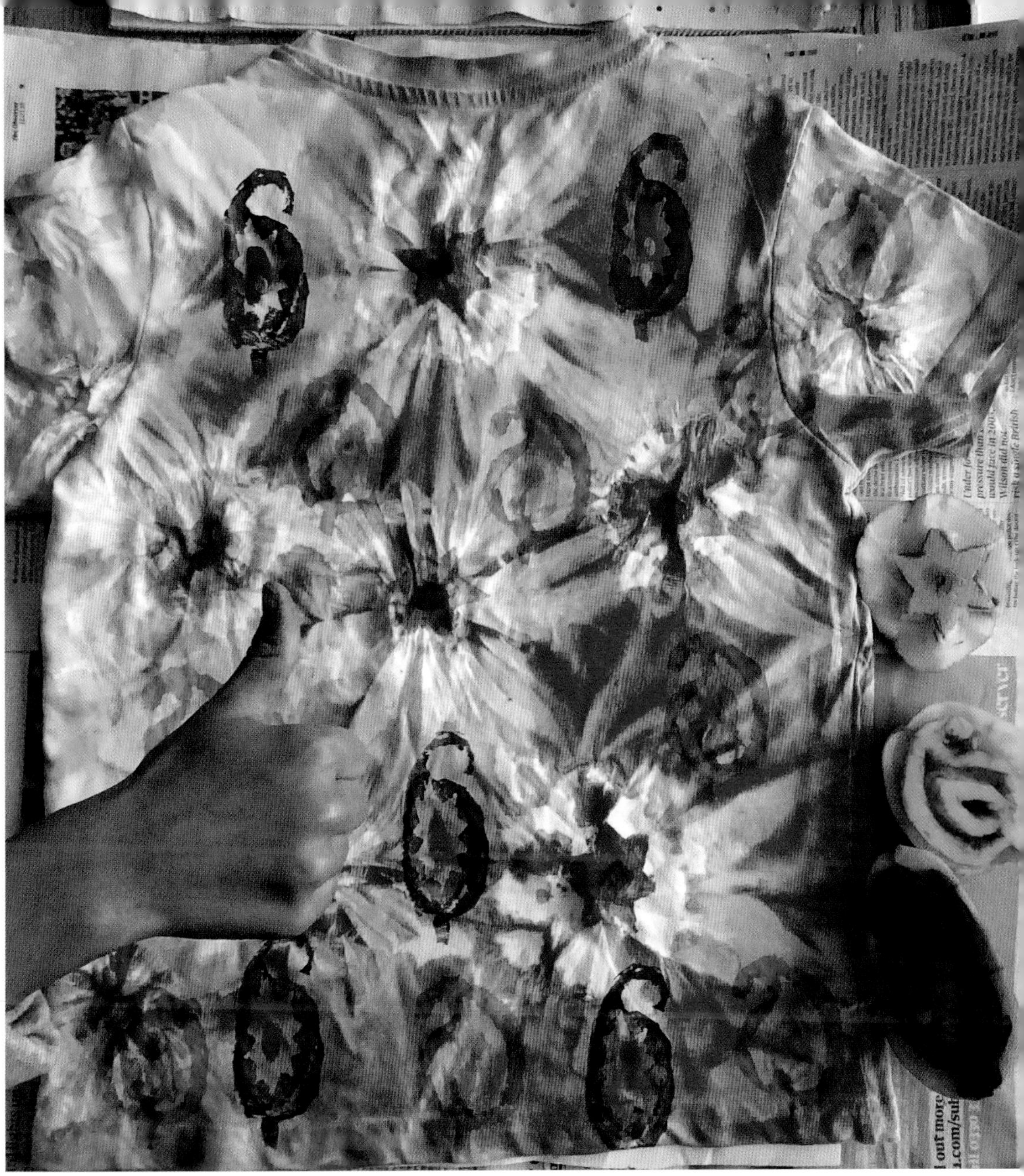

Above and Right While the T-shirt was drying – we laid it on paper on a warm radiator to hurry it along – we cut the potatoes with the Indian patterns. My grandson drew paisleys on two halves of a nice oval potato – two different designs facing opposite directions for variety. He then drew a roundish one and a star on the two halves of a rounder spud. I cut the more complicated patterns, following his drawing.

The dry T-shirt was ironed relatively flat, dressed in its paper lining and pinned out. We chose the colours of the prints to echo and enhance the colours of the bands – a good extra secret lesson in the use and effectiveness of both overprinting and colour itself. This part of the work was fun and messy; we had time to talk and discuss things, and to have little natural breaks for snacks while things dried. When both sides were completed, he decided some gold was needed to sparkle it up; luckily I had some gold fabric paint. This is usually quite viscous and easy to apply with a brush, which he did, adding dots round the neck, sleeves and hem as an extra detail.

Right His 'happy dance' says it all!

Chapter Twelve
FREEHAND PAINTING

Although I do use stencils, resists, tape and the other tools described to make patterns on cloth, most of my painting on textiles is, in fact, just freehand: brushes and colour meeting and meandering, running, hopping, rushing across the cloth, building pictures and patterns as I go. That's not to say I don't plan – I do. But I also allow for the design to develop almost as it needs to – the very fabric itself and the process of painting it plays such a big part in how the piece progresses. The following are examples of items I've made, which you could try versions of too; the methods and the thinking for each are indicated and described below.

Very often, a pattern actually demands something – these big plain discs were shouting for a lively fine red line.

EXAMPLES OF FREEHAND-PAINTED ITEMS

Baby's Coverlet

This small coverlet is a good example of a manageable size for a freehand-painting project.

Right I wanted to make quite a bold colourful floral but not have it too 'shouty', so I kept the flower heads light and warm, allowing quite a lot of the cloth to speak, and letting the background tell the main colour story.

Left The reverse is a simple marine blue foam dabber dot scattered on the natural cloth. By bringing it round to be sewn as the panel border on the front, the bright blue element is neatly framed and the feeling of lightness coming from the cloth colour itself is maintained. This dot is randomly spaced – though keeping the spacing even is not as easy as it sounds.

Tip

A helpful way to space out both these and the flowers (and to think about their colour distribution) is to cut or tear pieces of paper about the size you're planning, lay them on the cloth and see how it might work (see left for my paper flowers). When satisfied with the layouts, their positions can be marked with a fade-out pen.

Holly Bunting

Left This idea uses freehand painting a little differently. A while ago, on the back of a *papel picado* workshop I ran, I'd made some strings of cut-out paper leaves. These went nowhere, but the idea remained filed in my memory.

Top Left Years later, I've revisited this idea as part of my fabric bunting development plans. Strings of holly leaves to festoon the house seemed to me like the perfect Christmas decorations. Taking a piece of calico about 55cm (22in) wide and 65cm (26in) long, I set about painting the leaves. Each one is around 12cm (5in) wide and 25cm (10in) from leaf tip to stalk end. As you can see, they're rough and ready – very freehand indeed!

Left Each leaf requires two pieces so I painted another panel the same size for the back – this time with festive red dots. When dry, I laid them together, right sides out.

Top Right I then cut around the painted leaf shapes.

Bottom Right The holly leaves are sewn together around the raw edges (this is not couture!) with a central vein for stability and then attached by their stalks to a length of bias binding. I made several different strings, trying out various leaf colours and combinations. I also used the dotted remains as rather random danglers above my studio door.

LARGE-SCALE PAINTED PIECES

When it comes to painting large pieces, some of the important practical considerations are: how to space the motifs and how to keep their size consistent. Having worked on pattern repeats all my life, I'm aware of how easily these matters can slip. Photographing some of the large pieces for this book, I've had the chance to look at them from a distance, some for the first time. I've been rather pleased that for the most part they withstand this scrutiny – I actually work on quite a small surface and completing these big-scale lengths is almost an act of faith! You may feel adventurous too and want to paint on a big scale.

Unfinished Blue Length

I had a long piece of crisp new smooth *primissima* cotton and it seemed to need something large-scale on it. I fancied a limited colour palette for this – predominantly blues and indigoes – and a floral theme.

Left The shape of a magnificent bowl made by a friend had stuck in my mind. I realised the only way I could encompass this project and keep the drawing consistently to size and evenly spaced was to cut a paper template for the bowl. You can see that I've softly painted round it many times to give me a guide: a very simple and effective solution. Thus I have the framework for the composition and also the freedom required to paint the pattern.

Right Here is the panel in situ, the curves of the bowl elegantly echoed by those of the table.

Flower Vases on Invisible Shelves

Above This is another large panel, about 2.5m (8ft 2in) high, painted on a heavy creamy white linen.

Right I'd long admired Huw Morgan's Instagram posts for *Dig Delve*, which often showed a run of individual flowers in vases on a shelf. I began to think of painting something on that theme. Huw kindly sent me some more pictures to spur me on – here's one.

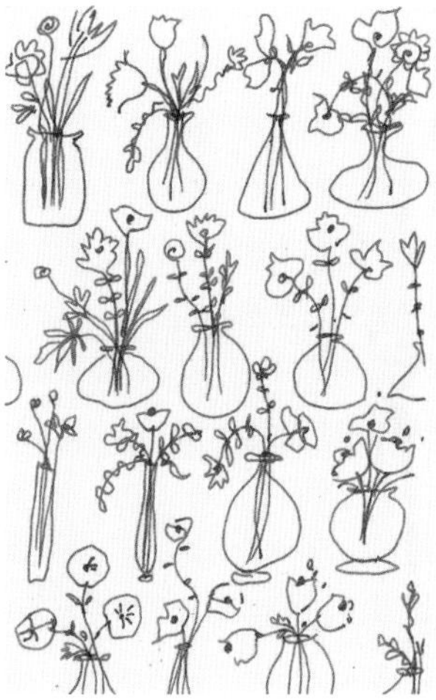

Above Here's the sketch of what I was thinking in my little A6 notebook.

Above Right In this panel the horizontal spacing was taken care of by the device of the implied shelves; to keep them straight, I ran a line of tape across the cloth, using a set square against the selvedge to make sure it was true. For the spacing of the vases themselves I ascertained the centre of the fabric and, using the span of my hand, placed them more or less evenly across. I used an auto-fade pen to mark my conclusions. I painted one 'shelf' first (the top one, I think) to understand the natural height of the filled flower vases and then spaced the other horizontals down the piece accordingly, one at a time.

Right Again, I used simple direct ways to divide a large space and make it manageable. Once the decision has been made to clear the decks and undertake a freehand painting of this size, I just want to get started. This was a case of trial and error in the painting. In the first version I made, above, the vases never seemed quite right – they were too pale and didn't balance well with the flowers; so I later painted over them with a brighter turquoise, which I think is more successful – one of the pleasing aspects of painting your own curtains! I'm afraid my flowers lack some of the elegance of those from Dan and Huw's garden.

Chapter Thirteen
PIECED AND PATCHED

BITS AND PIECES, SCRAPS AND LEFTOVERS

There are always pieces and scraps of painted and plain fabrics left over from projects, trials and samples. And scraps can be useful; to make the best of them some sewing may well be required – though not necessarily difficult or highly skilled. These examples are the sorts of things I think would be especially good to make with a companion or friend alongside.

Decorative Coat

When teaching courses, I paint a lot of demonstration pieces to show my techniques; I cut and made this coat from some of them using a commercial paper pattern as my guide. Planning what went where was dictated by the size of the bits of cloth I had. I tried to balance colours and motifs to give the whole thing unity.

The facings are made from the painting table backcloth, the pad fabric that happens beneath the painted silk hankies (see page 104). I had some interesting porcelain buttons handmade by a friend that needed a home; they were a perfect way to complete the outfit. You could make some special buttons quite easily with polymer clay.

Painted and Pieced Cushions

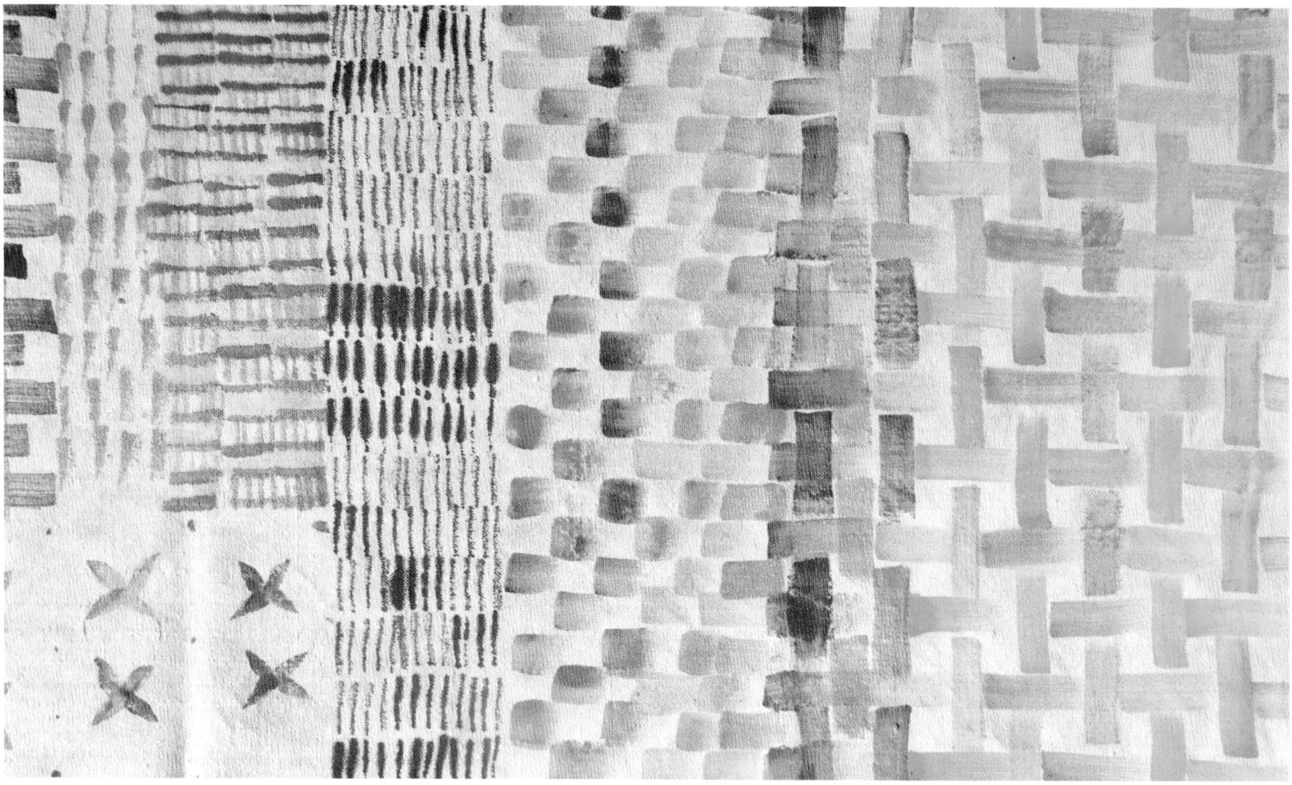

I had some remnants of old French linen bought at a *brocante* one summer – several different weights and sizes of cloth – that I then painted. I wasn't sure I liked them as big pieces so I cut them into smaller strips, shuffled them round and pieced them together into a long panel – and then wondered what to do with it! It hung around, literally, until I decided to make some cushions – there was just enough for two. Here they are below, sitting on a glorious old printed paisley shawl.

Triangle Bunting

Teaching in Mexico at the Hard to Find College in Guadalajara, I spent my day off making bunting for the classroom. For this I specifically painted a series of triangles on some scrap cloth and cut them out for the flags.

Less deliberately this triangular bunting uses ready-painted scrappy pieces of fabric, including the backcloth from my painting table. A 2.5m (8ft 2in) length of celebration flags took ten equilateral triangles at 18cm (7in) wide x 18cm (7in) deep to the point.

They are two-sided to give stability and full colour value, so twice as many need to be cut, machine-sewn together on two sides on the wrong side and then turned right side out. You could decide to make each run consistent – all speckles on one side and all stripes the other, say, depending on what you have available and what you might be celebrating. In this instance, mine are random.

The long edge of each triangle is then spaced equidistantly, caught and stitched with the machine into a folded length of bias binding. To space them out neatly, divide the amount of flags in half and starting from the mid-point of the string work towards either end.

Above Here it is, hanging in a corner of my room!

Pieced and Appliquéd Scraps Panel

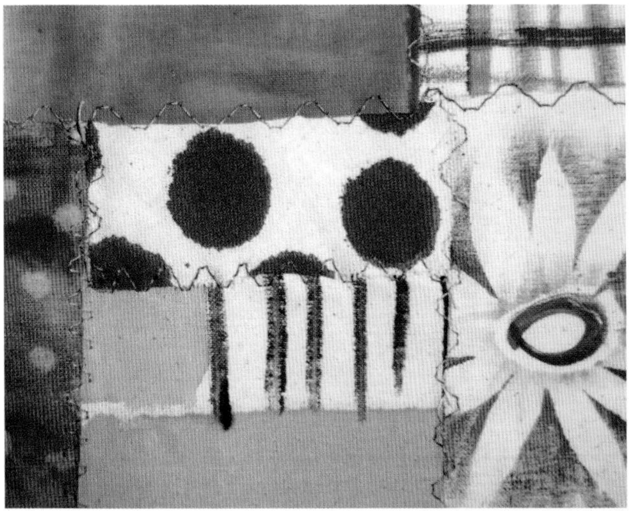

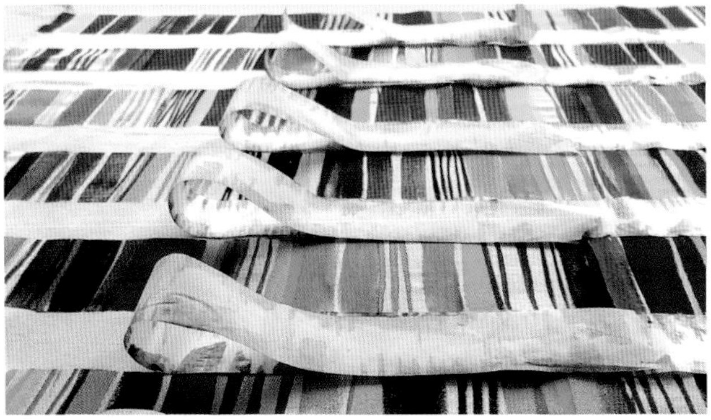

Another good, traditional use for scraps is, of course, as a patchwork. This panel is made from lots of irregular scrap pieces, some really small and fiddly. You could call it a 'lazy patch' as I made it more as an appliqué than a true stitched-together patchwork.

First I neatened the different fabric morsels, arranged them on a piece of fusible interlining and bit-by-bit carefully ironed them into place.

The interlining I had in my sewing basket was 1m (39in) square, and that was what I used. I then chose a wavey running stitch to machine sew each piece down and secure the raw edges. For this I used a space-dyed thread, making the colour variable, not intrusive. The deep edging pieces were painted especially for the piece, so don't strictly qualify as scraps.

To my eye, the edges needed some consistency, and I also liked the idea that the painted stripes themselves gave a nod to the fringes on a shawl. Masking tape kept the painting in order.

Stitched along each side, the binding strips hold the plain calico backing in place; a sandwich filling of a single layer of cotton batting in between gives the whole panel some weight and stability.

Little Rice Bag

This is a sweet little thing to make from small offcuts and scraps of ribbon. You can find how-to patterns for free on the internet.

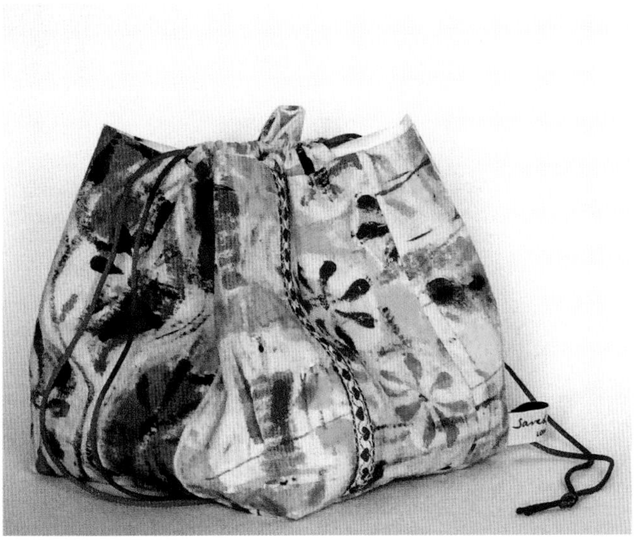

Wrapping Up

Many years ago I sent a huge roll of design work back from the States, wrapped in a printed flowery cloth from the collection I'd been printing – it looked lovely and arrived safely. Using fabric instead of paper is a great way to wrap presents, parcels and even picnics; and it's a good way to use up spare pieces of cloth. At Christmas and birthdays I gather various leftover pieces of unpainted calico and pin them adjacently across the table.

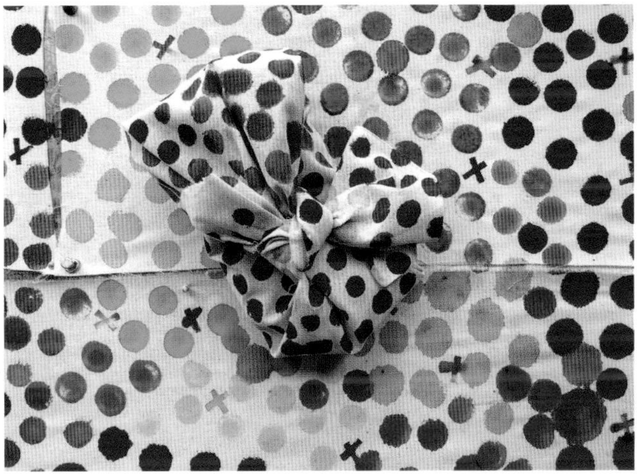

One year, taking my foam dabbers and a palette of assorted brightness, I decided to dot over everything! When dry and ironed I had a nice selection to wrap and fold around the various gifts. No sewing or sticking required, and everyone got the potential of a new hankie or bandana!

Wall Pockets

These are really useful! Usually made from a mix of what's to hand and specially painted, I have designed and sewn two or three wall pocket panels as presents for new babies. It makes for a very special and personal gift when names and dates can be recorded in paint.

Above and Top Right
These were made for two little brothers.

Right This panel is a personal record for myself.

Above When in Mexico I'd painted a jaunty stripe onto some very homespun cotton; I also saw lots of the famous traditional bright embroideries in the markets and bought some to bring home. I used them as inspiration to paint these small calico pieces.

Above Right With the painted stripe as a background fabric, I stitched the pieces on as pockets. The hanging loops use different scraps, and the whole piece is backed with a print from a furnishing fabric collection we designed in the 1980s; the hand-painted label records the date I made this panel. To me, the mix of fabric types adds to the notion that this piece remains as a record of that important journey and particular experience.

Things to consider when making a wall pocket panel: Is this for someone particular or a special event? Will it hang in a designated room or be destined for a specific purpose, for example for incoming mail for a family of five? Then decide accordingly on your: colour palette/theme, front, pockets, label, loops, backing (plain or patterned?) and interlining. Decide what you can use that's to hand and what you may need to paint for the occasion.

I've found a good size is around 58 x 76cm (23 x 30in), and five is a good number of pockets. When the pockets and ground are ready, I stitch the pockets to the front face and any label to the backing fabric and then place the back, front and interlining together, inside out (remembering to insert the hanging loops at the top and bottom). I stitch the whole lot together on three sides, leaving the bottom open for turning. Turn the 'bag' the right way round and topstitch the last side.

Right These are just two ordinary pockets made from leftovers and sewn onto a hand-painted shirt.

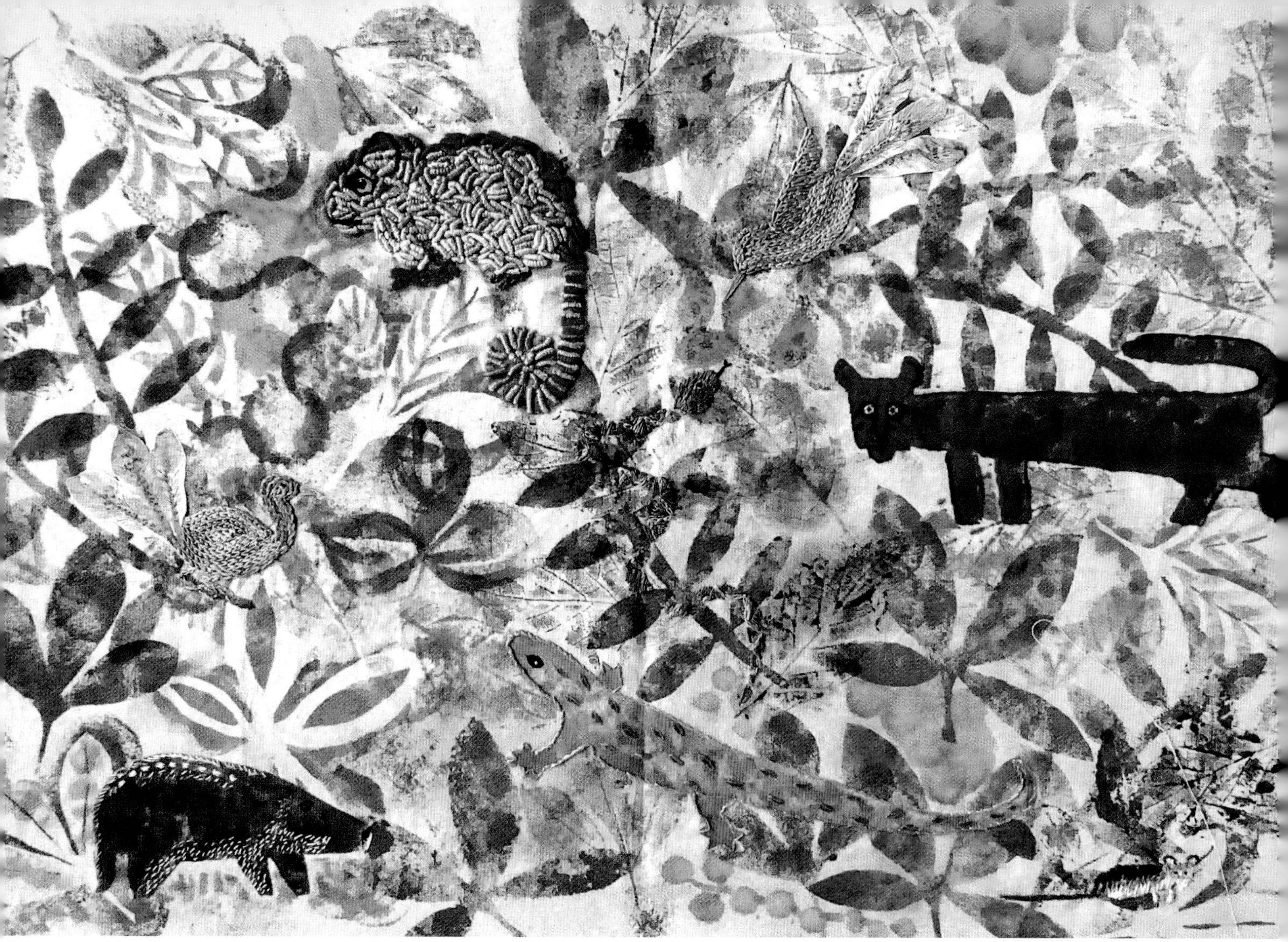

Chapter Fourteen

PAINTED FABRIC AS A BASE FOR DECORATIVE STITCHING

I often have students coming to my courses who want to make fabric as a basis for further embellishment and embroidery. They might be making decorative panels or clothing and are looking to make a textile to enhance and complement their scheme.

One student, Rachel Bowden, came with some friends who were all members of a local embroidery group. She worked hard over the three days of the course making a small panel using potato and leaf prints, painted marks and stencils.

A few months later, Rachel came to another course I was giving and brought her finished piece to show me. It was absolutely beautiful and original – I loved it. Sadly, Rachel died in early 2020, but her son-in-law has kindly given his permission for me to share my photographs of her panel here. I took these pictures quickly some time ago – they're the only record I have.

ANNIVERSARY PANEL

Hand-painted fabric enriched with stitch can make a beautiful present for a special person or occasion. I myself am not an embroiderer, but when my dear friends were about to celebrate their golden wedding I set about making something in their honour. They'd asked me for a poster to direct guests to their anniversary lunch, but I got a bit carried away! I had the idea to paint a fabric panel and depict at least some of the anniversaries and the gifts or tokens traditionally associated with them. It was really fun to make.

The painting itself was of a loosely gathered floral bunch, with the names and dates recorded on painted golden ribbons at top and bottom – a nod to the Trades Union banners we'd see together on marches and demonstrations in our youth.

Once it was painted and the colours set, I gathered little trinkets to stitch on, representing the anniversaries over the years. Different threads, ribbons and buttons were very helpful.

Top Right A flower cut from a baked beans tin for year ten.

Bottom Right A rosette of golden ribbons for the actual fifty!

Top Left A dollhouse newspaper for year one, the paper anniversary.

Bottom Left Flower petals picked out with wool for year seven.

Tip

To research more formal embroidery stitches and techniques, one good place to look is at the Royal School of Needlework. They really do have the fanciest confections in their fabulous Stitch Bank.

Chapter Fifteen THE THEATRE OF PATTERN

This book is not about learning to draw, to depict – I don't attempt to teach that. I draw almost every day of my life and in that particular I am fortunate; learning to look, see and record are important, but as I said at the beginning, representational drawing is not a prerequisite to making designs.

It's with a smile that I remember how my sister, Susan, and I sometimes performed impromptu little studio playlets, in which the characters were our colours: Yellow was always the noisiest one who insisted on hustling forward demanding attention. Black, on the other hand, was cool and still while allowing Red to flirt around him, showing off outrageously but getting nowhere. Blue looked on rather disapprovingly from afar while Green, a little exasperated with eyes cast up, waited for the flummery to die down before taking centre stage. These were the dramas of the colours. Painted fabrics, designs and garments can have a similar theatrical presence and purpose, particularly when specially commissioned. They set the scene.

CHRIS'S CHAIR: THE BEST SEAT IN THE HOUSE!

Over the years, friends have done me tremendous kindnesses; when I've asked how I can repay them, they've replied by asking me to paint something for them. This chair was just such an arrangement – as are Stafford's window blinds that follow.

I began, as usual, by mixing the colours and tried them out on a small spare piece of fabric to see how they'd behave. I applied colour very softly at first to give me the structure and build up my confidence too. I'd already decided to have a bird on what would be Chris's right shoulder as she sat, and I'd worked out how each of the panels would meet its neighbours so that the design would travel unbroken from plane to plane. Starting with the main focus, the interior back, I worked my way round.

Chris's chair had belonged to her grandfather. It was fairly respectably upholstered in a checked fabric, but she had recently moved into a new house and wanted everything in there to be beautiful and have a special meaning for her.

From the cloth samples she had, we favoured a natural-coloured linen fabric. She showed me a poster she really loves as a guide to colour and advised me of the general spirit she wanted – brightness and nature. As with all this sort of work, I cannot give a finish time – it so depends on my mood and the space on my table. Luckily Chris wasn't in a hurry as her house wasn't yet builder-free. Chris lined up Carol (her upholsterer) and we three agreed on the exact cloth; she then sent me individual pieces with the named shapes of the panels drawn on. One of each – no room for slip-ups.

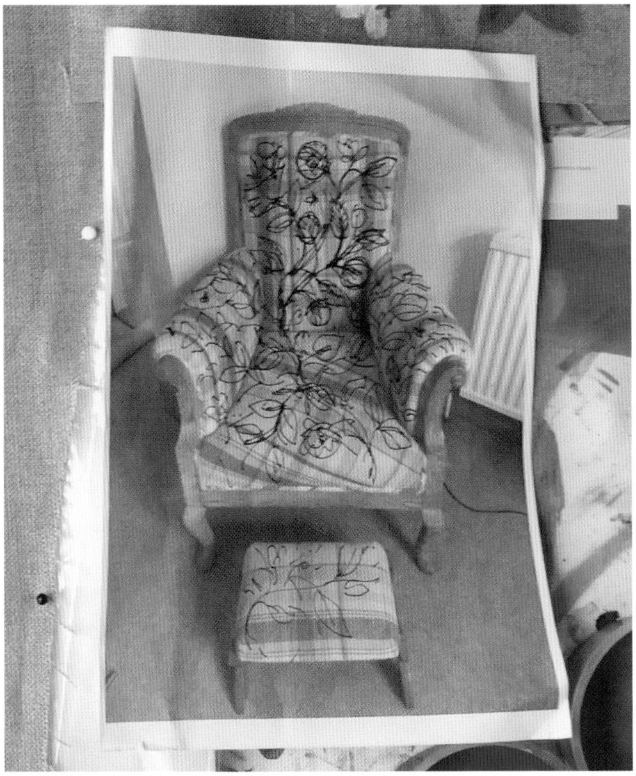

Above As often happens I had the idea in my head of what I wanted to paint – a branching tree with flowers, a bird, butterflies, bees, amphibians and ants (Chris's favourites). The only sketch I can find is this line drawing I made over the top of a photocopied picture of the original chair!

There were two areas undecided – the piping and the rear panel. It came to me that the double piping, acting as the defining edges, should be bold – black and white blocks. It was painted to be cut on the bias, and I did include quite a lot of ants but sadly they got lost in the make.

Above For the back, I used the same colours as on the front and painted a split stripe running across from shoulder to shoulder – simple and smart. Carol's upholstery was beautifully executed; I am so very pleased with the outcome – it was a wonderful commission and a triumph of teamwork.

STAFFORD'S WINDOW BLINDS: THE CHORUS

A few years ago, the author and designer Stafford Cliff asked me to paint some blinds for his kitchen windows. 'Of course,' said I, 'Do you have a theme in mind?' The windows opened onto a leafy front garden, and birds and trees were mentioned. This fabric was to be made in exchange for invaluable work he had done in friendship for and with me over the years, for which payment in actual money would have been impossible. I was happy to undertake such a commission.

When I enquired about the size of the windows, the email came back: 'Two side windows: 89cm (35in) wide; centre window: 114cm (45in) wide. All three windows: 236cm (93in) drop.' Painting these three long pieces of calico required some thought and planning.

To start with, I needed to have enough calico washed, ironed and cut to size – Stafford was going to make the roller blinds himself. I also needed to know that for the period of the commission, my time and studio table would be totally taken up by this one project.

I tend to think about a project like this for quite a while before I start, keeping the picture in my head rather than drawing a detailed sketch. I often don't know exactly how the painting itself will turn out but I need to have a strong feeling for the composition.

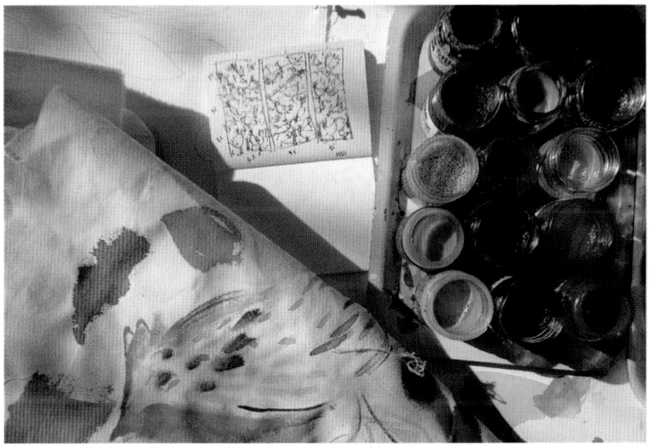

Above I made a tiny sketch as an indication of the sort of spacing and distribution I wanted over the panels. I then mixed some jars of paint.

Right Once I had pinned the fabric tight to the table, I began. This is the second panel in progress.

One of my main concerns about working over such a large area was to keep the scale consistent throughout – I didn't want giant birds dominating one area and tiny tweeters in another. As I have described on page 143, I mapped a very simple layout with the auto-fade pen, using the size of my hands as a guide to scatter the birds evenly across the pieces. I knew from experience that I could make their habitat of branches and leaves twine and grow around them as I went.

The birds themselves needed to be various in type, colour, habit and action, and I decided to give the panels a semblance of reality by having a grassy area at the bottom of each panel where birds could be standing. I consulted several of my bird books along the way. Above are the three panels hanging ceiling to floor in my flat, before they flew off.

JENNY'S CURTAINS: A QUARTET OF TREES

'To complement a country kitchen window with a leafy aspect and plenty of garden birds' – that was the brief. I decided these curtains, painted on linen, each needed two trees filled with flowers, leaves and birds – a certain formality allowing for spontaneous play too. The natural linen gave me the opportunity to include a white in the colour palette, which is a device I very much like. Again, the mapping out was crucial – the lengths were far longer than my table so I needed to paint them area by area. I painted these in two separate patches of time too, which meant mixing colours again and somehow getting back into the atmosphere of the painting and intention.

Sarah Campbell 2016

LAURA'S CURTAINS: A COUNTRY IDYLL

Of course, where there are curtains there's likely to be a window, and for this commission by a sister for a sister, I was sent a view that seemed to show a garden rising uphill from downstairs French doors. I don't know what came over me, but I really enjoyed this ebullient scenic painting. A fuller version of the curtains appear on page 9.

Left Somehow I felt impelled to represent a whole rural scene – paving, ponds, hills and sky, butterflies and dragonflies, feathers and fish!

Above Finding ways to depict 'reality' was interesting – after all nothing is real, yet we need to know the water is water, even though its pattern is a graphic device and the relative scale of things is quite questionable!

TWO 'OTHELLO' COATS AND OTHER COSTUMES

A friend who visits regularly from the US once brought me a challenge: she'd made up a calico (muslin, as it's called over there) toile of a very extraordinary and cunning pattern for a coat. It's called the Othello coat: the construction pattern for this particular item was created by Ruth Vincent, and initially inspired by photographs of garments made by Ruth E Funk, a US artist and philanthropist.

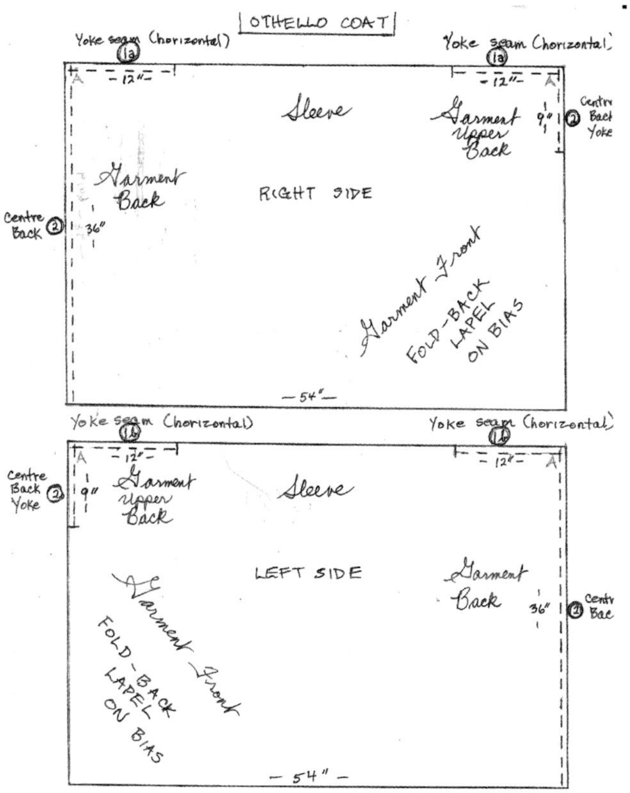

Left The toile sat in a pile for a year, and a couple of days before the friend next visited I fished it out and laid it flat on my kitchen table – it covered the whole expanse for the front and again for the back. I painted it as an abstract painting, starting on the back with the fine red vertical stripes that run across the shoulders. When one side was dry, I flipped the garment over to paint the front, making sure the front openings met nicely.

Above It drapes and hangs in quite a mysterious way, always giving a generous helping of pattern and colour.

I'VE PAINTED MANY OF MY OWN CLOTHES AND SOME FOR OTHERS

Above Left This Othello coat came in very handy for me to wear on a visit to Nottingham Contemporary to see their exhibition about the Bauhaus and its influences in September 2019.

Above Right I then developed the coat pattern a little to include pockets – an essential asset missing on the first toile. And, again, painting it was a question of laying it flat across the table and working through. This version of the garment is called 'Piano'.

Right I've painted many of my own clothes and some for others. At the start of 2020, I was invited by Inge and Hersilia at Livingstone Studio in Hampstead to make a little range of hand-painted clothes for their shop. It was a wonderful opportunity. Lockdown happened, but that didn't stop us! I painted away in South London on the pattern shapes we'd agreed, and I posted the pieces over to Chris who made them up in North London. She then cycled them round to Inge at the studio, and they contacted the customers they thought would be interested! It worked – here's a little selection of details on cotton, linen and calico.

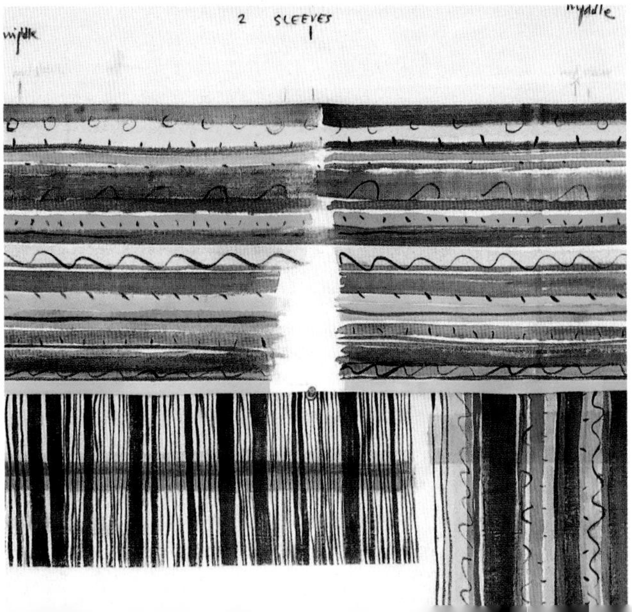
2 SLEEVES

POSITIVE/NEGATIVE: A DRAMA FOR TWO PLAYERS

Throughout this book I've mentioned pattern ideas that juxtapose positive and negative design elements, and the resulting play of two colours on a ground.

Left Almost at the start of my path into painting on textiles, I painted this silk scarf. It turned out to be a rich seam of design thought and development. It uses the cloth to shape silhouettes dancing out of a coloured ground with one other colour making areas of pattern – a simple and effective idea. It's one I love to use, as I have done in this calico panel opposite.

Right This large panel, 'Patterned Animals', is one of my most successful and well-loved pieces; full of life and variety yet such a simple design premise. Because it has been painted directly onto the cotton, the ground colour varies, the lines wobble and the patterning is a little uneven, but I think that adds to the charm.

Left This pattern, too, relies on the organisation of two colours on a ground; again using my favourites, red and black. This 'wandering vine' is a well-known motif in furnishing fabrics. Here I've set it out in such a way that the leaves and their respective backgrounds swap colours as they travel across the cloth, growing this way and that.

Right On this linen piece, the red and black have a graver significance. I painted this overnight after hearing Al Sharpton's eulogy for George Floyd in May 2020.

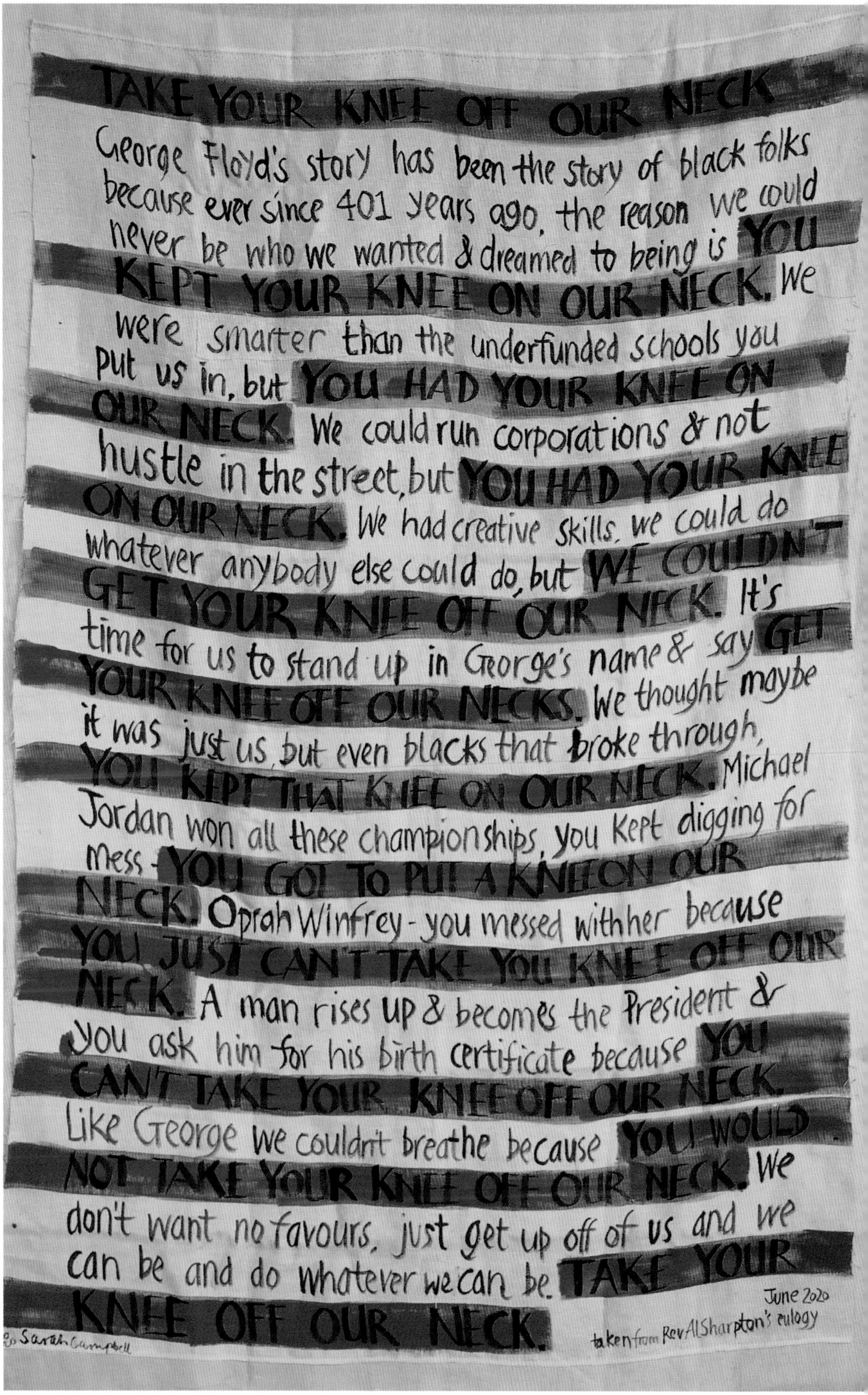

Conclusion

I hope the readers of this book have been encouraged to approach their own work with confidence and enthusiasm. Some direction has been given, and I hope taken; may at least some of the images, ideas, accounts and prompts ring true, give inspiration and be useful.

Acknowledgements

My thank yous are due...
To my family for their humorous and helpful support throughout this project, in particular to Joe, Rohan, Charlotte, Sophie, Lola and Rosa, and to Juana Lubian for all her tireless and enthusiastic help folding, ironing and wearing what I've been painting; to my late sister, with whom I worked for so many years and whose voice is still with me; to dear friends Vanessa, Stafford and Peter, who have nudged and occasionally kindly shoved me on my way; and to Alastair for lending his ears.

To all my students, who have taught me so much about teaching and learning.

To James Balston, who took so very many wonderful photographs, often amidst the working chaos of my flat, and to Peter Niczewski for stepping in and taking others.

To Chris Winter for sewing and designing garments, commissioning the armchair, and providing a lovely location; to Ruth Vincent for the use of the Othello pattern; to Charlotte Herxheimer for the loan of her painting '3 Potatoes' by Tony Beaver; to Noel Chapman (Japanese garments and stencils loan); and to Duncan Clarke (*Ndop* fabric).

For giving me the opportunity to paint some very special pieces – thanks go to George and his silk jacket; to Stafford Cliff and his blinds; to Jenny Shackleton and her curtains, and to Laura and Charlotte Ford and theirs (and to Isabel for photographing them – and me); to Vanessa and Sam Morton and their golden wedding anniversary; to Lola and Jamie and their wedding celebration chuppah; to Theo and Blake Hale, owners of the wall pockets.

To Rachel and Dan for the loan of their baby Robyn; to David Garland for the constant inspiration of his ceramics; to Livingstone Studio; to Poppy Frean for her cheerful, careful sewing; to Tom Bannatyne for kind permission to use images of Rachel Bowden's embroidered panel; to Huw Morgan and Dan Pearson for their flowers; to Sharon Everest for the exquisite little handmade dolls; to Anne Priest for her picture of me at Nottingham Contemporary; and to Brandon Mabley, who wanted a special T-shirt.

To Lucy Lloyd Davis for lending us her elegant house, and to Antenna Studios for other location shots.

Thank you to my very patient editors – Clare Martelli for commissioning this book and Tash Collin for seeing it through, and to Laura Woussen for designing it so cleverly.

And, lastly, to my three grandsons for keeping me on my toes!

The chapter headings are typeset in 'Elizabeth', designed by Elizabeth Friedländer, a German Jewish refugee and graphic artist whose life and work have long been championed by Pauline Paucker. That same Mrs Paucker was my art teacher when I was twelve – by good fortune, and after an interval of about sixty years, we met again very recently.

www.QueArts.com

Suppliers

UK

Atlantis
www.atlantisart.co.uk
Brushes and sundries.

Calico Laine
www.calicolaine.co.uk
Plain cotton wide-width sheeting, plus a wide range of calicoes and other fabrics.

Cass Art
www.cassart.co.uk
Brushes and sundries.

Cloth House
www.clothhouse.com
Dress-weight linens.

Cowling and Wilcox
www.cowlingandwilcox.com
Brushes and sundries.

George Weil & Sons
www.georgeweil.com
Fabric painting inks and paints, other fabric painting equipment, auto-fade pens, no-flow and resists, fabric by the meter, ready-made items, and always helpful advice over the phone.
01483 565800 / Old Portsmouth Rd, Peasmarsh, Guildford, GU3 1LZ.

HandPrinted
handprinted.co.uk
Own-brand fabric paints, selection of fabric painting inks and paints, other fabric painting equipment, no-flow and resists, fabric by the meter, ready-made items, and always helpful advice over the phone.
01243 696789 / 22 Arun Business Park, Shripney Road, Bognor Regis, PO22 9SX.

Hobbycraft
www.hobbycraft.co.uk
General craft supplies.

IKEA
www.ikea.com/gb/en
Simple calico and linen.

Jackson's
www.jacksonsart.com
Brushes and supplies, and a very informative website.

John Purcell Paper
www.johnpurcell.net
10mm foam board.
0207 7375199 / 15 Rumsey Road, London, SW9 0TR.

Royal & Langnickel
art.royalbrush.com
Brushes, foam brushes, dabbers and dobbers.

USA

NB: calico is often referred to as muslin in the USA.

Artist & Craftsman Supply
artistcraftsman.com
A good selection of fabric paints and other equipment. There are stores in many locations.

Blick Art Materials
www.dickblick.com
Fabric paint, foam board and sundries.

Dharma Trading Co.
www.dharmatrading.com
All supplies of inks, paints, fabrics and sundries.
1604 4th Street, San Rafael, CA 94901.

FLAX Art & Design
flaxart.com
San Francisco: *Fort Mason Center, 2 Marina Blvd, Bldg D, San Francisco, CA 94123.*
Oakland: *1501 Martin Luther King Jr Way (at 15th St.), Oakland, CA 94612.*

Jacquard
www.jacquardproducts.com
Inks, paints, fabric blanks and useful information.

JOANN
www.joann.com
Fabric, fabric paints and craft supplies.
There are stores in many locations.

Michaels
www.michaels.com
A good selection of fabric paints and other equipment. There are stores in many locations.

Needles Studio
www.needlesstudio.com
334 State Street, Los Altos, CA 94022.
Calico, linen, plain cotton and other fabrics.

US Art Supply
usartsupply.com
Foam brushes, brushes and general art equipment.

CANADA

Some of the USA stores also ship to Canada.

Curry's Artists' Materials
www.currys.com
Brushes, Pebeo fabric paints and inks.

King's Framing & Art Gallery
www.kingsframingandartgallery.com
General art supplies.

MAIWA
maiwa.com
Fabrics, blanks and meterage/yardage.

OPUS Framing & Art Supplies
opusartsupplies.com
Brushes, paints and art supplies.

AUSTRALIA

CraftOnline
www.craftonline.com.au
Fabric paints, brushes and sundries.

S&S Creativity unlimited
www.creativityunlimited.com.au
Fabrics, fabric paints, brushes and sundries.

Resources

Cosmetic sponges
From Superdrug or other chemists.

Reynolds kitchen freezer paper.

Jacquard inks and paints for fabrics.

Manila oiled stencil card
From good art shops.

Pebeo inks and paints for fabrics.

Swann Moreton scalpels and blades.

Tesa tape
From good decorators' merchants.

OTHER USEFUL LINKS

RSN world directory of stitch
rsnstitchbank.org

Furoshiki video tutorial
youtu.be/XxxW1pRHFcE